Gelligaer Histor

Founded 1

The Society aims to study local history
district of Gelligaer which includes the r
Bargoed, Hengoed, Ystrad Mynach, Tro
as well as the village of Gelligaer

GELLIGAER JOURNAL VOLUME 21

GREAT WAR EDITION
2014

Society Officers 2013-14

President	Islwyn Hughes	Treasurer	Greg Buick
Chair	Annie Owen	Committee	Nesta Jones
Vice Chair	Judith Jones		Dr. David Williams
Talks Organiser	David Mills		Ann Pinch

September - May monthly meetings with talk at Llancaiach Fawr.
All welcome.
AGM last Wednesday in June.
Details on www.gelligaerhistoricalsociety.co.uk

ISBN 978-0-9570426-2-9

Photo-montage on cover by Dr E.D.G. Williams

Contents

Notes on Contributors

David Carter, an elected councillor for Bargoed ward for ten years, is the current holder of the prestigious position of Mayor of Caerphilly County Borough. Born in Bargoed, educated at Lewis School Pengam and Open University, David has a wide range of interests ranging from sport, through music and literature to the environment, and spends much of his leisure time walking and enjoying the local scenery. Valentina, his wife of twenty one years, is an accomplished pianist, and together they attend St. Gwladys' Church.

Wayne David is the Labour MP for Caerphilly and Parliamentary Private Secretary to the Leader of the Labour Party. He was Wales Office Minister from 2008 to 2010. Wayne has been the Member of Parliament for Caerphilly since 2001 and from 1989 to 1999 he was the Member of the European Parliament for South Wales. In 2006 he published 'Remaining True' - a biography of Ness Edwards, the Member of Parliament for Caerphilly from 1939 to 1968.

Dic Felstead retired as deputy headteacher of Heolddu Comprehensive School in 2003. He has written several books on mythological and historical themes. Dic's biography of his grandfather "No Other Way - Jack Russia and the Spanish Civil War" (1981) was the first published memoir of a Welsh volunteer in that conflict. Dic's interest in the folklore and mythology of the old Rhymney Valley produced his current article in this journal. In 2013, Dic travelled to France to place a cross of remembrance on the grave of the young, aspiring writer, David Glyn Williams.

Audrey Griffiths. History was one of Audrey Griffiths' "A" level subjects and memories from those distant days include monarchies, dates and battles. Qualifying as an Official Wales Tourist Guide in 1986 and escorting visitors for the next 25 years changed her perception of history. Although Kings and Queens were important, visitors from other countries related more to the stories of ordinary people so now her passion is social history. She has developed a busy new career as a Speaker with a mix of subjects, serious and light-hearted. Those which are historical always relate to ordinary men and women and how they are affected. This is the ethos behind "The Home Front". She is a member of Gelligaer Historical Society.

Carol Henderson nee Price, born 1945, spent her early life in Church Road living with her parents and sister at Ty Catwg and her grandparents, at Ypres. She attended Gelligaer Infants School and Junior School and Lewis School for Girls. She regularly attended St Catwg's Church and was a member of the Parochial Church Council. She belonged to Gelligaer St John Ambulance Brigade and trained as a nurse at Caerphilly District Miners and East Glamorgan Hospitals She left the village in 1984 to nurse in Saudi Arabia and has spent most of the past 29 years nursing in the Middle East. She has 2 sons and 4 grandchildren.

Carwyn and Menna Hughes. Carwyn was brought up in Bedlinog and educated at Lewis School Pengam; Swansea and Southampton Universities and Carnegie College. Now retired, his career was in Secondary and Further Education. Menna was brought up in Bargoed and educated at the Grammar School and Cartrefle College. She has also retired and her career was in Primary Education. They are frequent visitors to France and are involved in the twinning of their village and a commune near Rouen, Normandy. Their project this year is to photograph graves and memorials of family members and men from Bedlinog who fell in Northern France in World War 1. They are members of Gelligaer Historical Society.

Judith Jones has lived for much of her life on a farm adjoining Gelligaer and Merthyr Common. After attending Bargoed Grammar School, she obtained a B.Sc. in geography at UC Swansea, and has subsequently studied on a part-time basis, gaining an M.A. in local history. Judith has taught in schools and in further education and worked in local government, but for most of her working life has been involved in farming. She is a long-time officer and member of Gelligaer Historical Society, editing and contributing to several of its journals. In 2003 she wrote a book about the Common.

Steven Kings Born in Field Street, Trelewis in 1956 into the Kings, Burley and Cunningham families, who had been long time inhabitants of the village but brought up in Treharris and still living there. Started work in 1975 for Merthyr Libraries before moving to Mid. Glam. Library Service in 1980 based in Caerphilly and then Bargoed and finally since local government reorganisation in 1996, Caerphilly County Borough Council Library Service. Through work developed an interest in family history and local history, though quite happy getting my hands dirty tinkering with my MG and my motorbikes.

Terry McCarthy was born Lytham St. Annes, grew up in Kent; Chislehurst, then Beckenham. In 1965 to University College Swansea to read Geography, Education and the Railway Magazine! Appointed assistant geography teacher, Lewis School Pengam, 1969, subsequently becoming Head of Geography, the Sixth Form, then Deputy Headteacher. 1999, appointed Headteacher at Bedwellty School, retiring 2004 when the school closed. Married Mary from Trelewis and Lewis Girls, 1973. Settled in Gilfach and had three children. Moved to Peterborough 2010 to be nearer the family. Continued researching and writing on south Wales railways, when not involved with U3A, Probus, Church and the grandchildren. He is a member of Gelligaer Historical Society and a former Chairman.

Annie Owen, member and current Chair of Gelligaer Historical Society, was born and brought up in Montgomeryshire. She read History in UCW Aberystwyth before entering the teaching profession. From the 1970s onwards and studying part time, she

4

gained further qualifications including both a Diploma and a Master's degree in Local History. She was awarded Cardiff University's Patricia Clark Memorial Prize in 2012/2013. She has been Editor in chief of publications produced by local historians on Taf Fechan, Fleur-de-lys and Bargoed and Gilfach.

Iris Owens. On leaving, Cardiff High School, accepted post in Foreign Office, London. She then took up teaching job in Switzerland. After three years at Alliance Francaise in Paris she gained a degree in French. On return to U.K she taught French in private schools in Cardiff. In a change of career she joined British Gas Wales in Network Analysis and Productivity Services departments and the Regional Training Centre. After early retirement she worked as a coach driver, while gaining an English Degree at University of Glamorgan. She worked as an EFL teacher at Ystrad Mynach College. She presents talks on historical subjects and travel. She is a member of Gelligaer Historical Society.

Neil Phillips. Brought up in Blackwood, Neil Phillips spent much of his early life with his grandparents, George and Doreen Owen, in East View, Bargoed. Neil is very proud of his Rhymney Valley heritage and still visits the area often walking with his two dogs through Gilfach, Bargoed and Aberbargoed and enjoying the pretty walks on the now landscaped old colliery site. Neil lives with his partner and two dogs near Newport, and although he has no children the family line continues through his niece and nephew, Romi and Jake, of whom he is very proud.

Marlene Shaw. Born in Gilfach in 1954, I was third of the four children of Myra and Thomas Chard. Our family moved to Bargoed when I was an infant. My father worked as a coalminer, painter/decorator and club steward, and my mother was a hairdresser. I was educated in Bargoed before studying secretarial and office duties at Ystrad Mynach College. My career has spanned various roles from secretary, seamstress, hairdresser, retail, catering and social services. I am passionately interested in local history, genealogy, literature, arts, crafts and music, while my two children and three grandchildren are my whole life.

Royston Smith. I grew up in the mining village of Brithdir, Rhymney Valley during 1946-66 then moved to Caerphilly when I got married. My working life commenced as an apprentice Mechanical Engineer with the NCB. Once qualified, I travelled the world with the Merchant Navy, and worked in the aircraft industry in various places including the Middle East. My passion for local history was ignited when I started tracing my family tree. In my desire to increase my knowledge I attended various history courses at Cardiff University being awarded the Elsie Pritchard Prize 2002 and attained the Certificate of Higher Education 2004. I am a member of Gelligaer Historical Society

Alun Watkins was born in Trelewis, attending the village school and Lewis' School, Pengam. At University College, Swansea, he graduated in History, later gaining a Master's degree in Education. He taught History in Grammar and Comprehensive Schools, eventually becoming Headmaster of two 11-18 Comprehensive Schools in Cheshire. Retiring to South Wales, his book, "A Village Headmaster" was published in 2013. This is a study of the life of John Davies (1851-1942), the longest serving Head of Trelewis School. Continuing to research aspects of the history of Trelewis has resulted in the current article.

Glyn Williams see page 72.

Foreword

I am delighted to commend this special edition of Gelligaer Historical Society's splendid journal. Its appearance, on the eve of the centenary of the official beginning of the First World War, on 4 August, is not only timely but an important contribution to the programme of commemorations which will extend over the next four years.

The centenary of the First World War is unusual because it is, in effect, a series of centenaries. It will also be different from many centenaries because the First World War touched the lives of every community, every institution and countless families across Britain and well beyond. This was, after all, a World War and during the next four years we will be reminded that while the Western Front saw the most dreadful and tragic encounters, there were military campaigns fought across the globe in which British soldiers were involved; Gallipoli, the Dardanelles, Palestine, Africa and even China.

While there will be major national commemorations of particular notable events and historical moments, much of the remembrance will focus on local communities and their own history such as the excellent programme developed by Gelligaer Historical Society. Over the next four years, building on work already well under way, we shall see the production of significant educational resources, especially through the digitisation of artefacts of all kind including diaries, letters and photographs, together with a series of local projects funded by the Heritage Lottery Fund and other funders which will help to fill the gaps in local knowledge. Local memorials will, in many cases, be renovated and the collective memory of towns and villages will be recalled. New internet sites have been created for this purpose and these will provide an enduring legacy for the study of the war and its impact.

That impact extends beyond the military campaigns into the economic and social effort on the Home Front and the huge changes which were wrought in politics and society. While those who lost their lives in the war have, quite naturally, occupied front-stage in remembrance, there will be an opportunity to consider the impact of the war on those who survived and, in many cases, continued to suffer. Many men were unable to fight – some because their occupations and professions were deemed to be more important in support of the war. Others resisted the war on grounds of conscience, one of the most notable of whom was Morgan Jones, later MP for Caerphilly, and the subject of an article in this journal. That war, moreover, went a considerable way to promoting the cause of women's rights culminating, in 1918, in the partial extension of the franchise to women, completed in 1929. Much of this spectrum of change is reflected in the articles in this edition of the journal.

Societies like Gelligaer Historical Society will play a crucial important role in developing the programmes and projects of commemoration. Local history will be every bit as important as national institutional history in explaining the impact of the war. The personal experiences of young men who had, in many cases, never left their home village only to find themselves hundreds of miles away in a foreign land facing appalling circumstances, will be a vital reminder of the harsh reality – that war is fought by ordinary people who, often, have no choice in the matter.

I would also like to pay tribute to the Committee and the officers who have, over many years, helped to enrich our understanding of the history of this important industrial community not least through the long series of the Journal. Through publishing an enduring historical memoir such as this, we can help the present and future generations to understand more fully the experience of the nation as a whole.

Deian Hopkin

Professor Sir Deian Hopkin is President of the National Library of Wales and Expert Adviser to the First Minister of Wales on the Centenary commemorations of the First World War. A former Vice-chancellor of London South Bank University he also spent 24 years at the History Department at Aberystwyth and was founding editor of Llafur, the Journal of Welsh People's History.

Introduction

Dedicated to the memory of everyone associated with this area during the Great War era, *Gelligaer Volume 21 Great War 2014* is part of Gelligaer Historical Society's commemoration of a horrific conflict that not only touched communities and families countrywide, but also left an indelible mark on the lives of both contemporaries and generations to come. This modest volume aims to complement similar projects, locally and nationally, in contributing towards a better understanding and appreciation of a global war that still leaves its mark on today's society.

The story of the war is complex and far-reaching, and there are as many different aspects of that story as there were people. For some, war was leaving family and friends and familiar streets for the hell that was a battle in a foreign place with an unpronounceable name. Some of those people did not return, while others came back as broken people. While not everyone who left home ended up on the front line of battle, the experiences of those who served in offices or factories are just as much part of the war story, as were those of people who stayed at home. To some people, the war meant spending spare time serving on the village *Welcome Home Committee* or knitting *comforts* for local servicemen. The war for young wives in new communities like Bargoed was often a bewildering experience as they worried about absent servicemen husbands while struggling to bring up children without the support of an extended family. For many young children it was getting to know the stranger who was their father when the war was over. Whatever the experience, the war changed people. The injustice, pain and mutilation witnessed by nurses, servicemen and communities like those mentioned in this volume influenced social, economic and political expectations in the post-war era.

The Society is indebted to contributors, both Society members and friends, who have devoted so much time and effort to the thorough research reflected in the pages that follow. While the help and support of many, including librarians and archivists, is greatly appreciated, it would not be invidious to mention Greg Buick, Society Treasurer and Webmaster, whose skill and patience in preparing the draft for the printer has ensured that this volume sees the light of day.

Gelligaer Historical Society is also researching names on local war memorials and the result of the research into the war stories of those who made the ultimate sacrifice is on the Society's website. It is a work in progress and the Society will be pleased to hear from anyone who can supply additional relevant information and/or photographs, or who knows of memorials in local places of worship or other public buildings.

There are still many untold war experiences within the former Gelligaer Urban District and it is hoped that not only will contributors to this journal continue their valuable research work, but also other people will feel inspired to find out more about their family or community during the Great War.

Testament of Youth
Dic Felstead

Winchester of Wales

David Lloyd George MP was the guest of honour at the official opening of the refurbished Lewis Boys' School in 1904.

In his speech he articulated his hope that the Pengam School would become the Eton or Winchester of Wales. This was no kindly gesture, rather a statement of distinct possibility. Firmly rooted in a tradition that spanned two centuries, Pengam Grammar School had its eyes firmly fixed on an illustrious future.

Thomas Matthews

Because of its reputation, the school was able to attract teachers of the highest quality, and none more so than Mr Thomas Matthews MA of Llandybie, Carmarthenshire, who joined the school in 1911 as Welsh and Geography master. An author with wide cultural interests, Mr Matthews soon set his own scholastic stamp on the school.

Llen Gwerin Blaenau Rhymni

He instructed his pupils to go out into the community, to collect and record whatever legends were part of the area's oral tradition. The fruit of the boys' researches was published in book form in 1912 entitled *Llen Gwerin Blaenau Rhymni (Folk Tales of the Rhymney Valley),* and it contained a collection of hitherto unpublished folklore and nursery rhymes current in the district. Upon publication the book attracted much attention, being adopted by some schools in the Principality as a Welsh Reader, and receiving very favourable press notices.

The first section of the book which contained some twenty legends was the fruit of the endeavours of eleven young authors, two of whom would soon be fighting in the First World War.

Levi Emrys Williams of New Tredegar studied at Lewis School between 1909 and 1914 and was responsible for *Tylwyth Teg yn Nyffryn Rhymni (The Rhymney Fairies)*, a tale of how a frustrated farmer tamed a troupe of mischievous fairies who plundered his stock.

David Glyn Williams of Gilfach Bargoed who attended the school between 1910 and 1913, authored three of the 20 legends. These represent the most eloquent and mature of the collection and are unique in the history of folklore. *Cawr Gilfach-Fargoed (The Giant of Gilfach-Fargoed)* and *Glo Cyntaf Cwm Rhymni (Rhymney Valley's First Coal)*, taken together, represent the only legends in British folklore which deal with the discovery of coal. He tells how an alliance of fairies, local farm labourers and an owl, fed up of the cruelty of a giant, devised a plan for his destruction. In disposing of his body, their fire revealed the existence of coal beneath the ground. David's *Capel Gwladys* is a beautiful love story explaining the origins of the chapel which lies above Bargoed on Gelligaer Common.

The Gathering Storm

Soon, however, storm clouds began to gather and blacken the European skies and the infernal deluge began on 28-July-1914.

Lewis School faced many difficulties during the following years of conflict due to a depleted staff and governing body having gone to war. In 1914 the school established a Cadet Corps in order that those boys who were called up would have had the chance of a period of training in readiness. From Christmas 1914, the number of "Old Boys" who joined the Forces increased rapidly and it is estimated that some 500 Lewis pupils participated in the struggle from the start of the war to Armistice. Forty-five of them, nearly ten per cent, gave their lives for their country, some of them merely boys ripening into manhood.

Dail y Gwanwyn

In 1916, the school published another book entitled *Dail y Gwanwyn (Leaves of Spring),* consisting of essays on various subjects in Welsh. In the opening paragraph of *Dail y Gwanwyn* Thomas Matthews explains that the intention of the publication was to donate all its profit to the *Ysbyty Cymreig,* the Welsh Hospital. The book sold freely despite the dislocation caused by war and profits eventually amounted to £28.

Welsh Hospital

The Royal Victoria Military Hospital based in Netley near Southampton opened its wards in 1863 after Queen Victoria voiced grave concerns about the dreadful conditions soldiers faced in Crimea during that conflict and ordered a military hospital to be built in  Britain. Its proximity to the coast meant that hospital ships from around the Empire could safely dock and disembark its wounded.

In 1914, the Netley facility was expanded by erecting large Red Cross huts

in the surrounding fields to accommodate growing needs. This was the location of the so-called Welsh Hospital, established to treat military personnel from Wales and funded by voluntary contributions from the Principality. The Welsh Hospital provided an extra 1,500 beds for the treatment and recuperation of its patients.

THE WILLIAMS BOYS GO TO WAR

- **Levi Emrys Williams**

Levi Emrys enlisted on 27-July-1915 but was discharged invalided in July 1916. In June 1917, he returned to action joining the Royal Naval Air Service, the air arm of the Royal Navy before it amalgamated with the Royal Flying Corps to form the Royal Air Force. Levi Emrys saw action in France as a pilot during August of that year and after just two months was promoted to Squadron Commander.

In March 1918, he was brought down by a shell whilst bombing the German lines and was badly wounded by shrapnel. For his gallantry he was recommended for the *Croix de Guerre*. The Croix de Guerre, Cross of War, was a French military decoration, first created in 1915, and commonly bestowed on foreign military forces allied to France, awarded to individuals who distinguished themselves by acts of heroism involving combat with the enemy.

Levi Emrys was the only young author to feature in both of the Lewis School publications. In *Dail y Gwanwyn,* his contribution secures prime position by being the first to appear in the volume and its title *Cyffes Maboed (Testament of Youth)* seeks to deliberately highlight the thoughts of a young man embarking on a journey through a dangerous world. The book also carries a picture of him puttee-proud in military uniform.

CYFFES MABOED

R'wyf ond pererin
Bach,eiddil, a gwan,
Parhau wnaf I deithio
Er cyrhaedd gwyn fan:
Croes wyntoedd y ddaear
A chwyth lawer pryd,
Ond Duw a ofala
Am danaf o hyd.

Mae'r croesau a ddeuant
Yn erbyn sant gwan,
Yn ddigon i'w rwystro
I ddringoi i'r lan;
Ond dringo raid imi
I fyny'n ddibaid,
Heb feddwl am gefnu
Pwy bynnag ddwed – "Paid."

Tra bwyf yn yr ysgol,
Rhaid cofio bob dydd,
Bod dysgu y gwersi
Yn ddyled a budd;
Rhaid parchu yr athraw
A phrisio ei waith,
Am geisio fy nysgu
Tra yma ar daith.
                    Emrys Williams

TESTAMENT OF YOUTH

A young pilgrim, that's me
Somewhat fragile and weak,
But onward will I plod
To reach that place unique:
The cross-winds of the world
Mightily they blow,
But God will care for me
That much I know.

Stiff challenges will come
To test a weak waif,
Sufficient to hinder
His quest to be safe;
But endeavour I must
Without losing hope,
Without a waiver
To show that I can cope.

Every day I should praise
The worth of learning
And remember that study
Is a true blessing;
I must value my school
And honour my tutor
For his firm resolve
In framing my future.
                    Dic Felstead

- **David Glyn Williams**

David Glyn Williams joined up on 16-April-1917 as a Private in the 3rd Battalion of the Welsh Fusiliers. He was at the Western Front on 15-August-1917 during the Third Battle of Ypres or Passchendaele, a name that has become synonymous with the nightmarish pornography of war. He was killed in action on the 31-August at the age of eighteen years and is thrice remembered:

✓ Cement House Cemetery is located in Langemark, Belgian Flanders, four miles north of the town of Ypres. The village was in German hands from April 1915 to August 1917, the month when David lost his life. Cement House is the military name given to a fortified farmhouse which housed the original cemetery containing an irregular group of 231 graves that was begun at the end of August 1917. Private David Glyn Williams, 61432, who fought with the 14th Battalion Welsh Fusiliers, son of David and Elizabeth Williams of Gilfach Street, Bargoed, dead at  eighteen years of age is remembered with honour here.

✓ At the end of the war, it was decided to erect a brass memorial tablet in the Assembly Hall of Lewis Boys' School. A subscription list was opened and the tablet engraved to a Celtic pattern contains the names of the forty-five young men whom the school wished to honour. Amongst their number is David Glyn Williams. The dedication and unveiling took place on 30-April-1920 and was conducted by the Rev. T. J. Jones, Rector of Gelligaer in the presence of a large audience of school staff and pupils, parents and relatives of the fallen youngsters. The plaque can now be viewed in the foyer of the new Lewis School, Pengam.

✓ The name of David Glyn Williams is commemorated on Bargoed War Memorial which was constructed by public donation and originally located at Hanbury Square. It was unveiled in June 1923. The memorial was relocated in Bargoed Park in the 1960s. Subsequently it was moved to its current position within the grounds of St Gwladys Church on 11- November - 2007. It is a very fitting location for young author of Capel Gwladys, a story that transforms enmity into love.

David Glyn Williams, however, outlived his literary mentor and school master. Thomas Matthews, the inspiring teacher who enabled the creative talents of his students, passed away in September 1916 after a long and painful illness. Without his guidance and the youthful enthusiastic storytelling of students like David Glyn and Levi Emrys, the legends of the Rhymney Valley would have died too.

SOURCES

- Commonwealth War Graves Commission   Cement House Cemetery
- Felstead, Richard   Myth and Folklore in the Parish of Gelligaer   Gelligaer Historical Society 1982
- Felstead, Richard   From Mouths of Men : the roots of story   Dragon's Tale   Vol 2   1985
- Felstead, Richard   Legends and Folk Tales of Rhymney Valley Rhymney Valley District Council   1986
- Matthews, Thomas (ed)   Llen Gwerin Blaenau Rhymni   Lewis Boys' School. Pengam   1912
- Matthews, Thomas (ed)   Dail y Gwanwyn   Lewis Boys' School   1916
- Wright, Arthur   The History of Lewis School, Pengam   Welsh Outlook Press   1929

The Young Authors of Llen Gwerin, 1912
David Glyn is seated in the front row, far left. Levi Emrys is in the back row, far right.

14

Gwenllian Lewis, nursing in the Territorial Force Nursing Service, WW1

Judith Jones

Gwen, as she was known, was born on 13th January 1881 on her family's tenanted, small upland farm, Clwydtrawscae, near Bedlinog, the sixth of the twelve children of Daniel Lewis and his wife Ann. Her upbringing, typical of the time, must have been hard. Farm income from the 63 acres had to support the family, pay the rent and pay the farm bills so there would have been very little surplus cash. Water had to be carried about 80 yards from a well on the nearby mountainside and there were many jobs that an older sister would have done, such as milking the cows, helping with the care and feeding of the animals and with the harvest, as well as helping in the house and helping care for the younger children. Nevertheless, Gwen and her elder sister, Mary, were lucky as they had an education at Pontlottyn Girls School (the forerunner of Hengoed County School, later Lewis Girls School, Ystrad Mynach). Mary then trained and became a school teacher, while in September 1904, Gwen went to train as a nurse for three years at Swansea General and Eye Hospital where she qualified on 19th September 1907.

She left Swansea, continuing her training and qualifying as a staff nurse at the Belvedere Hospital in Glasgow, then between January 1911 and 30th September 1913 Gwen worked at the Institution of Trained Nurses for the town and county of Leicester before transferring to the 5th General Northern Hospital, Leicester.

Information on the University of Leicester website tells us about this hospital. It describes how the University was *founded as a Memorial to the local men who died in the First World War* and how the current main administration building started life as an asylum which was re-located in

1910. The website continues,

In 1911 the empty County Asylum building was identified by Medical Officers from the Territorial Force or TF (predecessor to the Territorial Army) as a suitable location for a military hospital, should the need arise. . . Three years later that need did arise and the building was designated as the base for a TF medical unit, the 5th Northern General Hospital. Outbuildings were demolished and replaced with four long, flat-roofed brick huts to house officers while nurses and medical staff had rooms in the main building.

Information on the University's website also explains that the 5th Northern General was not just the name of a building but was a major medical corps unit which occupied a number of other buildings in the area. As detailed in Gwen's wartime records at the National Archives (WO/399/12761), it was to this unit that she became attached when "called up" on 4th November 1914 to become a nurse in the Territorial Force Nursing Service (T.F.N.S.).

Sue Light, on her website scarlettfinders.co.uk, explains that the only nursing organisation which had been specifically devoted to the (regular) military was the Army Nursing Service, created in 1881 and which was changed in 1902 to what was then known as the Queen Alexandra Imperial Military Nursing Service (QAIMNS). This Service however, was originally filled with women from a high social status – although this criteria was removed during WW1. Sue Light also describes how the T.F.N.S. was formed in 1908 as a result of the Territorial and Reserve Forces Act of 1907 to provide a nursing service for the Territorial Force, and it was anticipated that these nurses would staff the twenty-three TF general hospitals planned for the United Kingdom in the event of war. She describes how the women who enrolled in the service from 1909 were civilian nurses who continued to work in their usual capacity, but had undertaken to be mobilised at short notice in case of war, writing,

2,760 women, who in peacetime went about their normal duties in civil hospitals and private homes, but with a commitment to the War Office and holding mobilization orders . . . The Standing Orders for the T.F.N.S. closely mirrored those of QAIMNS, and the standards of entry were similar. The insistence on a full three year nurse training in an approved hospital remained, though it seems likely that when appointing staff, rather more emphasis was put on professional ability than on social standing. . .

Although originally intended for home service only, in 1913 members of the T.F.N.S. were given the opportunity to notify their intention of

Staff at Trouville, France. Gwenllian Lewis is sitting in the middle at the front.

willingness to serve overseas if required, and the sudden need for a large number of nurses to accompany the British Expeditionary Force to France in 1914 resulted in some members proceeding overseas during the early weeks of the war.

The majority of nurses in the T.F.N.S. however, spent most of the war years in the United Kingdom and for most of this period Gwen remained at the 5th Northern Hospital where she nursed men who had been returned from service in France. Her annual reports described her as a *quiet methodical medical nurse,* although the Matron-in-Chief did not *consider ... she has a strong enough personality to be fitted for promotion.* Nevertheless, the British Journal of Nursing of 31st March 1917 records that on 23rd February 1917, Gwen was honoured to be one of four staff nurses of the T.F.N.S. who was decorated with the Royal Red Cross by King George at Buckingham Palace.

On 10th March 1917, she signed an agreement to be sent abroad to nurse, giving the name of her brother, Thomas Lewis (who had taken over the tenancy of Clwydtrawscae), as her closest relative. On 20th February 1918 Gwen went to France and served in a field hospital, the 73rd General Hospital, British Expeditionary Force at Trouville. She returned to Folkstone and was demobbed on 3rd August 1919. At the end of her military service Gwen's testimonial, signed by the Matron-in-Chief of T.F.N.S., Sidney Browne, reads

All her reports are good. Her professional qualifications, her ability to teach others and train orderlies are up to the average, and she is very kind to her patients. Miss Lewis is a quiet, very methodical worker, and an excellent medical nurse. Her influence is invariably good,

Gwen continued to nurse. She returned to the 5th Northern General until March 1921 when she left, married a doctor, Jamie Young, and they subsequently moved to Cambridge. They never had children - but never failed to send much anticipated book tokens at Christmas to Gwen's great-nieces at Clwydtrawscae, Jamie continuing to do so after her death in 1959.

I am not aware that anything which Gwen wrote or said about her work during WW1 has survived, but much that was written for her or about her has survived - in her autograph book for the period between October 1914 and October 1918 while she was serving in Leicester and in France.

The majority of the book's entries are expressions of thanks for the care given by the nurses. 2nd Lieutenant F. Cuthbert Tonkin of 7th East Yorkshire Regiment's pen and ink drawing, for example, showed how much he appreciated the hospital and staff.

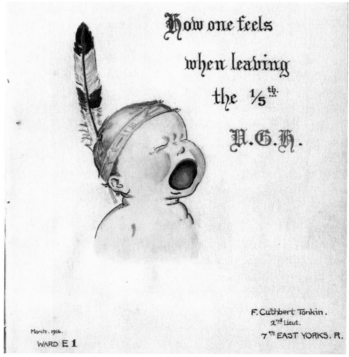

How one feels when leaving the ⅕[th.] N.G.H.

March . 1916.
WARD E 1

F. Cuthbert Tonkin.
2nd Lieut.
7th EAST YORKS. R.

There were also many personal compliments to individual nurses, including Gwen, such as the entry by (bilingual) Captain I. L. Stevens of the 63rd Regiment de Ligne, 11th Bataillon, who wrote,

There is a young lady from Wales,
The land of mountains and vales,
With the sweet soothing smile,
That helps all the while,
To cheer up the soldier that ails.

followed by,

Blessé au Coeur le 26 ^e Novembre 1915 d'une fleche de Cupid,
Quelle blessure ne se guerrira jamais.

(Wounded in my heart 26th November 1915 by Cupid's arrow, a wound that will never be healed)

The men - from Britain, France, Belgium, Australia, Canada and New Zealand – often mentioned the battles in which they had fought. Private F. Johnson of the 3rd Cavalry Brigade, 16th Queen's Lancers, for example, wrote that he had been at Mons, Aisne, Marne, Soissons and Ypres before being wounded at Warneton. He added, *"Just come to see what is doing in England soon be on the move again with the Old 16th."* They described their injuries, mainly bullet wounds, bayonet wounds and frostbite. One who suffered from frostbite was W. H. David of 403 Somerset Yeomen who drew a picture of the Kaiser and the devil with the label Comrades in Arms while recovering at Leicester in December 1914. From their descriptions of where and how injured, it is clear that in most cases, men were brought back to Leicester within two to four days of being wounded.

A fascinating insight into people, everyday life and attitudes in Ward E1 at the 5th General Hospital can be found in 2nd Lieutenant, Army Service Corps, J. Rodger Haldane's The ABC of Ward E1 Leicester base Hospital, April – May 1916; "I" referring to the building's former use and illustrating the disillusion and cynicism of the serving men.

A's for Appendix which Carter & Co.,
Pant after as hart after water brook; so
B's for the Bismuth they'll give you (don't laugh)
And X-ray your tummy and say "yes; we'll strafe".
C's for a Colonel who can't stand a noise,
So silence for once is imposed on the choys.
D stands for "Dug-out" a V. A. D. makes,
By drawing a screen round your bed in two shakes.
E stands for Evans, the sister so kind,
Who mothers us all with such patience of mind.

The
A B C
of
Ward E 1, Leicester Base Hospital,
april — May, 1916

A's for appendix which Carter & Co.,
Pant after as hart after waterbrook; so

B's for the Bismuth they'll give you (don't laugh)
And X-ray your tummy and say "yes; will staff"

C's for a Colonel who can't stand a noise,
So silence for once is imposed on the bhoys.

D stands for "Dug-out" a C. A. D. makes,
By drawing a screen round your bed in two shakes,

E stands for Evans the Sister so kind
Who mothers us all with such patience of mind.

F stands for Farrington; golf gives him fame.
He's lucky at "bingt-et" or any old game.

G stands for "Grand" where, I'm told by a few,
The bhoys often go. I don't think so. Do you?

H stands for Hughes, parries bayonets by hand;
Who's heart's rather troubled but appetite'sgrand.

I's for the Inmates, once wrong in the head,
Now placed on the Staff of the Army 'tis said.

J stands for juice squeezed from lemons each day
For drinks for the patients so festive and gay.

K stands for Kodaks and photos they take
And work they find Sisters with prints that they make

L stands for Lineham, the "little bit of Heaven",
The strong C. A. D. who's eleven stone seven.

*F stands for Farrington; golf gives him fame,
He's lucky at "vingt et" or any old game.
G stands for "Grand" where, I'm told by a few,
The choys often go. I don't think so, do you?
H stands for Hughes, parries bayonets by hand;
Whose heart's rather troubled but appetite's grand.*

I's for the Inmates, once wrong in the head,
Now placed on the Staff of the Army 'tis said.
J stands for Juice squeezed from lemons each day,
For drinks for the patients so festive and gay.
K stands for Kodaks and photos they take,
And work they find sisters with prints that they make.
L stands for Lineham, the "little bit of heaven",
The strong V. A. D. who's eleven stone seven.
M's for the Mesopotamian Mess,
Which good Sister Brown will do much to redress.
N's for the Nurses who are gems one and all,
And all looked so sweet at their Christmas-time Ball.
O's Operation which Burnburlidge does,
With maximum skill but with minimum fuss.
P stands for Porter who smokes cigarettes,
The major so patient who sleeps n' nor frets.
Q stands for Queen; that's what happened, but stay;
I'll tell you that story some other fine day.
R stands for Records, both hymnal and gay,
A broken-down gramophone sometimes can play.
S stands for Sowter, a ray of the sun,
Called "Ginger" and "Blossom", but second to none.
T's the "Thermometer, clinical one",
Nurse Sadler each morn leaves for hours on your tongue.
U's for Umbrella with which Sister Sue,
Adorned the veranda (and Sister Brown too).
V's for Von Cooke, he of Downington Hall,
And V.A.D. sisters, he loves one and all.
W stands for Wales, famed for mountains and girls;
Nurse Lewis was born there, she's one of its pearls.
X is the things that the patients all say,
When medical boards say they must go away.
Y is for Your's Truly who'll often recall,
The unnumbered kindnesses rendered by all,
Z's for the place where we'll all be next year;
So here's to good luck. May it ever be near.

(V.A.D.s were the Voluntary Aid Detachments, choys - non-nursing ancillary workers)

Patriotism and the fervour for war were shown by some. In May 1916, 2nd Lieutenant Christopher Ley of the South Notts Hussars, for example, wrote a poem which he attributes to Jessie Pope (although I have not been able to verify this)

> *For England*
> *Before the cloud broke overhead*
> *And spat its jagged flame:*
> *We drank and revelled, laughed and fed,*
> *And England was a name.*
> *But now that one and all are burnt*
> *With War's relentless hand:*
> *By that same token we have learnt*
> *How much we love our land.*
>
> *Our little land of sun and rain,*
> *Our land of grey and green,*
> *The stubble field, the shady lane,*
> *Each old familiar scene,*
> *Our rocky coastline closely bound*
> *By restless billowing waves,*
> *And in hushed nooks of hallowed ground*
> *The dear sequestered graves*
>
> *For this our Fathers lived and died:*
> *For this they shed their blood;*
> *For this and for our Empire wide,*
> *They faced both flame and flood:*
> *THIS is the heritage they handed down to us,*
> *For this we face the strife:*
> *Stands ENGLAND where she did? She does,*
> *And SHALL while we have life!*

Later Christopher Francis Aden Ley served as a Captain in the Royal Flying Corps, but was killed on 16th March 1918 and buried in his home churchyard at Leaholme, Danby Parish, North Yorkshire, where his name is engraved on the church roll of honour.

More well-known nationalistic verses were such as those written in Gwen's book by Private E. A. Baxter of the 4th Leicestershire Regiment in December 1914,

> *On land and sea as brothers we*
> *United true shall dauntless stand*
> *Our motto be Britannia Free*
> *True sons of Empire hand in hand*

and Private L. Piggott of the 2nd Battalion VHRR[1] in January 1915,

---

[1] Very High Readiness Reserve

> *Today our hearts to those we love incline*
> *For Empire, King and Auld Lang Syne*

Cynicism – or realism – was already creeping in. In the same month, C. H. F. Pritchard of the Royal Berkshire Regiment wrote,

> *Little Willie went a fighting*
> *On a summers day*
> *But winter came and bit his toes*
> *They carried him away*

Many pictures were included. For example, Captain John Turner of the 8th Battalion, Royal Warwickshire Regiment drew a watercolour of the coast and sea (location unknown) while in the field hospital near Trouville.

He returned to the front, and his papers, deposited at the Imperial War Museum (WO/374/69915) (also quoted in Robert David Williams, "A Social and Military History of the 1/8th Battalion the Royal Warwickshire Regiment in the Great War" University of Birmingham thesis, 1999), reveal his conflicting and changed attitude towards the war. In his horrific account of the Battle to secure four lines of German trenches in an area between the villages of Beaumont Hamel and Serre on 1st July 1916, he noted, w*e went over first . . . followed by crowds of famous regiments. The 8th were splendid . . . past imagination . . . the regulars and the generals cannot say enough for the dash and spirit of our onrush.* The truth of the onslaught emerged in his description of the return journey, *Oh that awful journey, the dead and the dying lying, crawling along the ground. Oh my God, dear God.* Turner later wrote home, *the 8th that you knew is a memory only . . . 45 out of 600 answered the roll at 11 a.m.*

The Regiment was re-built and later fought at the Somme and 3rd battle at Ypres, Passchendaele; John Turner's name on the Roll of Honour in All Saints Parish Church, Clevedon shows that he was killed in action at the Battle of the Selle, 22nd October 1918 and has no known grave.

Nevertheless, the patients showed that they retained their sense of humour.

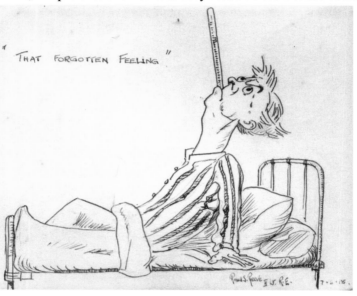

2nd Lieutenant Russell S. Reeve drew this in June 1918 while in hospital at Trouville. He later won acclaim in the field of art, but it was at this time, during WW1, that his drawings came to the attention of other artists who suggested that he attend the Slade School of Art at the end of the war

Many similar autograph books have survived, so in this, as many other ways, Gwenllian Lewis was typical of those thousands of women who nursed the military during WW1; women about whom relatively little has been written, whose work is largely invisible and forgotten, and yet was invaluable. On her website, Sue Light quotes Dame Maud McCarthy, Matron-in-Chief of the T.F.N.S. (she had held the same position with QAIMNS during the war) who in 1920 describes the T.F.N.S. nurses as a *noble band of women, ably officered, admirably chosen, rising to heights of skill and endurance unguessed at by any at the outset of war.* The little evidence offered above suggests the accuracy of this statement.

Nurse Rose Smith

Annie Owen

Nurse Rose Smith, formerly a nurse in Gelligaer's Isolation Hospital, arrived at London's Waterloo Station on February 12 1916 after some five months war service overseas. That evening, the *Merthyr Express* reporter recognised her, in her grey and white headdress and with red cross on her sleeve, on the Cardiff to Rhymney train, and his account of her war work appeared in *Merthyr Express* February 19 1916.

Having left for Serbia with a group from Scottish Women's Hospital (SWH) under Drs. Elsie Inglis and Alice Hutchinson on September 11 1915, she arrived in Malta on September 18 before embarking for Athens, a place that thrilled her with its beauty.

The party of nurses was divided into two groups to go to Serbia to nurse wounded Serbians. While there, Nurse Smith was impressed by the fortitude of the Serbians as well as their strong devotion and love of their country. Although at first, the brave Serbians felt that help had arrived too late and that the British nurses would leave when troubles started, the nurses shared the hardships and dangers and continued to work in spite of enemy bombardment. From October 11 to November 10 1915 they were at Kraguevatz, but when invaders forced them to leave, they went to Krushevatz where they remained until December 28 1915. Nurse Smith recalled that a fine body of Germans marched into Krushevatz, sang their victory song, hoisted the German flag and forced the British nurses to leave as German nurses took over the nursing work

Having left Krushevatz, the British nurses travelled via Semenuria and Belgrade, a city in ruins, to Kevivara (in Hungary) where they slept on straw, twenty nurses to a room. Leaving Kevivara on January 6 1916, they were told they could return home and journeyed via Budapest to Vienna, where they were informed they would be interned because the Allies had arrested Consuls in Salonika. They appealed to the American Minister who helped them with money and ensured their accommodation in a good hotel. Nurse Smith was impressed with the beauty of Vienna and the seemingly happy life there. From Vienna the nurses went to Weidhofen where they were split into small groups and quartered in different houses, confined to walking within a radius of ¾ mile and forced to report to the police station daily to receive 5 kronen to cover cost of living. After being thus interned for about a month, they were sent back to Vienna where they met thirty five other members of the Scottish Women's Hospital from Serbia who had fared less well.

Nurse Smith and her colleagues travelled home via Switzerland, where, at

Berne, not only were they were warmly received by the American Minister, but also presented with bouquets by ladies, while people thanked them for what they had done in Serbia. They enjoyed the sights in Berne before crowds assembled to give them a warm send-off on the express train to Paris. Dr. Hutchinson, producing a hidden Union Jack, waved it as the assembled crowd cheered when the train left the station. After a night in Paris, they left on February 11, travelling via Le Havre to Southampton, before boarding the train to arrive at Waterloo Station on February 12.

Merthyr Express, March 11 1916, carried a report on a local public reception in recognition of Nurse Smith's war work. It started at Aberbargoed Station at 5.30 pm when she was heralded by discharge of a detonator and a party of Cheshires and Monmouthshires under Sergeant James fired a salute. Nurse Smith was welcomed by Rees Davies, Chairman of the Local Reception Committee, Rev. T. Richards, B.A., vicar of Bargoed, Ben Rees of Aberbargoed, Organising Secretary and Captain of the District Ambulance Brigade, and Mrs W. Ebsworth, Commandant of the local Red Cross Brigade. Representatives of many local organisations, including Fire Brigade, Red Cross Brigade, Ambulance Brigade, Church Lads Brigade, Boy Scouts and Girl Guides, as well as contingents of servicemen, formed a procession with Nurse Rose Smith, accompanied by Rev. T. Richards and his young daughter, and Rees Davies, travelling in an open carriage. Large crowds gathered along the route to cheer her gallant actions as the procession made its way through Aberbargoed, Pengam and Fleur-de-lys before returning to Nurse Smith's home town of Bargoed. On reaching Bargoed's Trafalgar Square, Nurse Smith was cheered and applauded and the Vicar spoke of the area's pride in honouring her. A modest Nurse Smith simply replied *I thank you all very much*.

The wartime contribution of women like Nurse Rose Smith was important not only in helping to alleviate suffering but also in encouraging change in the public image of women in Britain and in raising respect for the professional skills of nurses. According to *Merthyr Express*, Nurse Rose Smith volunteered for further wartime nursing duties, but sources studied to date have not shed light on it.

What made this public reception and procession different from the majority of such events reported in detail in the pages of wartime issues of local newspapers, was that the large crowds were cheering a female, a nurse, rather than a male serviceman.

Morgan Jones and the First World War

Wayne David

Morgan Jones was born on 3 May, 1885 in the village of Gelligaer at the foot of Gelligaer mountain. His birthplace was the small Rhos Cottages, close to the ancient parish church of St Catwg. The cottages were to remain his boyhood home.

Morgan Jones' father, Elias Jones, was a local collier, born in the hamlet of Llanwonno, near Mountain Ash. He was known for his sobriety, his dependability and his hard work. His mother, Sarah Ann, originally from the village of Llanfabon, was a strong and formidable woman with an earthy sense of humour and bright blue eyes. It is said that Sarah Ann had worked as a young woman in Llancaiach Fawr, the local Tudor manor house. What is certainly true is that she had a far from easy life at her own home, tending livestock as well as carrying-out her other domestic chores.

In the Jones household, Welsh was the language of the hearth, liberalism was its politics and Protestant non-conformity, of the Baptist variety, was its religion. Sarah Ann was especially devout and helped imbue in the young Morgan a strong religious belief. Indeed, of the seven children – two girls and five boys – it was Morgan who became the main focus of her attention and her encouragement. She recognised that of all the children it was Morgan who had the greatest ability and potential.

After attending Gelligaer and Hengoed Elementary Schools, Morgan won a scholarship to Lewis School, Pengam. He matriculated from Lewis School in 1901 and began training as a pupil teacher in Gilfach Boys' School,

Bargoed. From there he gained admission to Reading University and studied 'Education and the Arts'.

In 1907, Morgan returned to the Rhymney Valley. He went back to Gilfach Boys' School as a teacher and continued the lay preaching which he had begun as a student in Reading. But if Morgan's religious non-conformity had been reinforced by his university experience, his politics had now firmly moved to the left. In 1908 Morgan joined the Independent Labour Party (ILP) and helped establish the Rhymney Valley's first branch.

In South Wales the political dominance of the Liberal Party and its working class offshoot, Lib-Labism, was now under threat from a new radicalism which was sweeping the South Wales coalfield. It was the ILP which was at the forefront of the challenge.

In March 1911, Morgan Jones threw his hat into the political ring and stood for election to Gelligaer Urban District Council (UDC), describing himself as a 'socialist'. With a majority of only 11 votes Morgan Jones was elected and soon proved to be an effective and committed councillor, making housing his pre-occupation. In fact, due largely to Morgan Jones' efforts, Gelligaer UDC became one of the most forward looking local authorities in South Wales, building quality council houses throughout its area, but especially in Bargoed.

On Gelligaer UDC Morgan Jones put municipal socialism into practice. His democratic socialism was firmly based on a materialist analysis of capitalism, combined with a strong sense of moral purpose, which drew much from his religious non-conformity. In essence, Morgan Jones was a Christian Socialist.

Equally central to his beliefs was his conviction that nations and peoples ought to live in harmony with each other, respecting difference and celebrating diversity. For Morgan Jones it followed that international disputes must always be solved through diplomacy and dialogue rather than through armed conflict. As a pacifist he believed that warfare could never be justified.

When Britain entered the First World War in August 1914 Morgan Jones was in no doubt that this was a conflict which was wrong. Like many in the ILP, Morgan Jones believed that war generally, and this war in particular, could not be justified. True to his convictions, he argued that the disputes between the European powers should be resolved through discussion without resorting to arms. From the beginning of the war Morgan Jones therefore linked up with the likes of Bertrand Russell and Fenner Brockway, and when the No Conscription Fellowship (NCF) was formed in late 1914 Morgan Jones was appointed to its National Committee. He later became Chairman of the South Wales Anti-Conscription Council.

During the first half of the war, until 1916, the army consisted entirely of volunteers. The country was awash with jingoism and the leadership of the South Wales Miners' Federation (SWMF) was amongst the most enthusiastic for the war effort. In Bargoed Labour Exchange alone there were 1,315 recruits in the first three months of the war. In such a climate, by opposing the war, Morgan Jones was seen by many as nothing less than a traitor.

By the end of 1915 there had been half a million British casualties and the horrors of the war were becoming increasingly clear. With the declining number of volunteers the Government felt that it had to introduce conscription to maintain the war effort. Accordingly, in January 1916 the Government introduced the Military Service Act. This meant that all unmarried adult men up to the age of 41 were regarded as being enlisted in the armed forces, even if they had not received their call-up papers, and therefore subject to military law. In May 1916 the measures were extended to cover married men as well.

A hierarchy of Tribunals was set up to decide if an individual who was a conscientious objector to the war could be given 'alternative' employment or if they should be given a custodial sentence if they refused. Gelligaer UDC was informed by the Government in January 1916 that it would be expected to convene a local Tribunal. At roughly the same time Morgan Jones received his call-up papers. It soon became clear that the Council Tribunal would be expected to consider the case of one of its own members.

At a full council meeting in February 1916, with Morgan Jones present, the Council voted by only ten votes to eight to uphold the law and give the Chairman and the Clerk powers to convene a special council meeting as necessary. A special meeting was in fact called soon after, but it was inquorate; it seems that the "Labour" councillors deliberately boycotted the meeting. But not to be thwarted, those councillors who did attend formed themselves into a 'committee', augmented by a local doctor and a Justice of the Peace, and this body became the local Tribunal.

Morgan Jones was summoned to appear before this Tribunal after he refused to respond to his call-up. As happened throughout the country, after the war the Government ordered that the records of the Tribunals be destroyed. This was the case with the Gelligaer Local Tribunal and explains the gap in the otherwise unbroken minutes of Gelligaer UDC in the

Glamorgan Archives. However, the local press covered the meeting of the Tribunal at which Morgan Jones appeared and provided an account.

In a packed courtroom in Bargoed, Morgan Jones told the Tribunal that he was a "socialist" and was "resolutely opposed to all warfare". He went on to say that, in his view, the war was the product of "wrong-headed diplomacy". The local Tribunal came to the conclusion that Morgan Jones could be excluded from military service, but not from alternative service. Morgan Jones was not prepared to accept this and therefore appealed to an Appeals Tribunal in Cardiff. His appeal was unsuccessful and on 29 May 1916 Morgan Jones was arrested at his parents' home in Bargoed.

At about 8:30am the local police inspector called and asked to see Morgan. According to Morgan, the police officer was "most courteous and polite" and made him feel "quite at home", although Morgan was concerned that his mother "was somewhat alarmed" when the police officer arrived. After being arrested, Morgan was taken to Bargoed Police Station and later that day the police raided the ILP offices in the town.

From Bargoed, Morgan was taken to Cardiff where he appeared before the Magistrates Court. He was fined 2/- and sentenced to four months imprisonment for refusing to obey military orders. He was taken to Cardiff Gaol.

At the same time as the police took action in South Wales, the leadership of the NCF was also the subject of a police crackdown in London. As Morgan Jones was waiting to be arrested in Bargoed, other members of the NCF National Committee were appearing before magistrates in the Mansion House in London. Eight members of the National Committee, including Morgan Jones in his absence, were found guilty of prejudicing recruitment by circulating a leaflet calling for the repeal of the Military Service Act. They were each fined £100, the maximum possible, plus £10 costs, and if they did not pay the fines they were each to face 61 days imprisonment.

A month later, the National Committee members appealed against the judgement and Morgan Jones was brought up to London from Cardiff Gaol, escorted by two policemen. He appeared before the court with his fellow Committee members and although he "looked white and worn", he presented his case and responded to the questions asked of him "with great spirit and determination". Morgan Jones explained to the court that he had been kept in solitary confinement for three weeks, but despite the hardship he had faced he had "no doubt" about the stand he was taking.

As expected, the appeal was rejected and the convicted were given 14 days to pay their fines or face imprisonment. Most of them went to prison.

On the day after his arrest in Bargoed, as well as appearing before Cardiff Magistrates, Morgan Jones was also brought before Caerphilly Magistrates Court. Here, on 30 May 1916, he was found guilty of being an 'absentee', was fined £2 and it was decided that he would be placed in the hands of the military. He was kept in detention of one form or other until the end of 1917.

After Caerphilly Magistrates, Morgan Jones had to face a military court martial. Even though he had never served in the armed forces, under the Military Service Act he was found guilty of "desertion" and sentenced to a period of "sheer hard labour" with the military. He began his sentence at the Kinmel Park Army Camp in North Wales, but was then transferred to join other conscientious objectors in Wormwood Scrubs.

It is difficult to appreciate the hardship which Morgan Jones experienced while in prison. There were periods of solitary confinement and throughout Morgan survived on a poor diet and was the subject of constant personal abuse. Within a few months Morgan's physical and mental health deteriorated, and in November 1916 Morgan re-evaluated the nature of his conscientious objection. As a result, he no longer felt able to uphold the 'maximalist' position as an absolute conscientious objector and instead he became an 'alternativist'. This meant that he was breaking ranks with the leadership of the NCF by being prepared to accept 'work' which did not involve bearing arms but which nevertheless could be seen by some as indirectly contributing to the war effort. Morgan's view was that it was important to differentiate between armed conflict, which he remained opposed to, and the legitimate functioning of the state.

From his prison cell in Wormwood Scrubs and then from his room in the Home Office Work Centre at Warwick to which he was transferred, Morgan Jones made an effort to explain and rationalise the change in his position. During 1917 he engaged in correspondence with Mansell Grenfell from South Wales who remained a prisoner in Wormwood Scrubs, and before that Morgan corresponded with Clifford Allen, the Chairman of the NCF, who also remained in Wormwood Scrubs.

In an undated letter to Clifford Allen, which seems to have been written in late November 1916, Morgan Jones, however, did not make any real attempt to defend the alternativist position which he had adopted. He stated that "it would be pointless and profitless for me to enter a discussion of the 'Alternativist and Absolutist' business now. We will not emphasise differences. Let us rather emphasise agreements. And in one way at least we are certainly at one – to work together each in his own way to realise the Co-operative Commonwealth of the future".

The letter to Clifford Allen also is interesting because it explained that the experience of imprisonment had reinforced Morgan Jones' religious beliefs. "More and more," he wrote, "I am compelled to recognise and appreciate the value of individual character and the formative influence of religion".

The second reason why the letter is of interest is because it contains Morgan Jones' heartfelt concern about his family back in South Wales. One of his brothers had received his call-up papers and there was very real worry that because of his ill health he would "fail to survive the war". Another of Morgan Jones' brothers was also a conscientious objector and had been forced to leave his teaching post. Morgan Jones was always very close to his mother and he was extremely concerned that the pressures that his family were facing would "prove too much for her". A final worry for Morgan Jones was whether his engagement to his fiancée would last. In fact, it did not.

An earlier letter to Catherine Marshall, the Secretary of the NCF, written soon after Morgan Jones had been transferred to Warwick, shows even more clearly the psychological strain which Morgan had been subjected to in Wormwood Scrubs. In the letter he explained that "the effect of prison" had been to take away his ability to concentrate "upon any subject for any length of time". He said that his mind was in a "nebulous condition" and that sometimes he felt his scalp was "about to fly off".

In the Warwick Work Centre, Morgan's health continued to worsen and because of this he was released at the end of 1917. But this did not mean the end of his agitational work and in April 1919 Morgan appeared before Bargoed Magistrates charged with desertion, even though the war had ended some five months earlier. Even more bizarrely, he was charged with deserting from the Lancashire Fusiliers. It appears that after granting him bail at £10, the Magistrates handed him over to the military and the authorities contrived to keep him under lock and key for a further three months. This time he remained in detention until 2 August 1919.

Morgan Jones' conscientious objection to the war meant that after the conflict had ended he was prevented from returning to school teaching. Despite his ill health, he worked for a time as a labourer in a local colliery before becoming the ILP's Welsh Organiser and joining the National Council of the ILP. He remained a member of Gelligaer UDC throughout the war and following the Armistice, when he was able, he returned to his council work.

In March 1919, Morgan unsuccessfully stood for election to Glamorgan County Council when he contested the Bargoed ward. But in December

1919 he was elected in a by-election following the death of a councillor who was a local Congregational Minister. At the first meeting of the County Council after his election, Morgan Jones was collectively and individually snubbed with no welcome or congratulations being offered to him by the Chairman of the Council or any of his fellow councillors.

Morgan Jones had taken a principled stand against the First World War. He and his family suffered enormously and Morgan Jones himself was subjected to terrible ill-treatment while in prison. Indeed, the physical strain which those years imposed on him was to remain with Morgan throughout his life and almost certainly contributed to his premature death at the age of 53.

The huge trauma of the First World War left a deep scar on the country, not least in South Wales. The heady jingoism of the first few months of the war steadily gave way to a sense of resignation as the death toll mounted. But this did not mean that the public hostility to Morgan Jones diminished. If anything it increased as the war dragged on. After the war there were inevitably raw emotions as so many had lost loved ones. Increasingly though, Morgan Jones' contemporaries came to question whether such a conflict had been necessary and what it had achieved.

In July 1921, Alfred Onions, the strongly pro-war Labour MP for Caerphilly, died after a period of illness. Against the backdrop of economic crisis, Morgan Jones won the support of the local miners, who rejected their leaders' advice, and secured the Labour nomination. The following month saw Morgan Jones win a stunning and overwhelming by-election victory, thereby becoming the first conscientious objector to be elected to Parliament.

Morgan Jones had made a courageous stand against an appalling conflict. He did what he believed to be right. His election showed that even those who had bitterly disagreed with his stance at the time, nevertheless, were prepared to support him as a man of principle who was determined to help create a better world, free from war.

Note on Sources

Much of the information for this piece has been gleaned from newspapers. The *Caerphilly Journal* and the *Merthyr Express* have been particularly rich sources, complemented by the ILP paper *Labour Leader*. These have been especially important because of the destruction of the documentation from the Tribunals and Gelligaer UDC. John Sheaff, the son-in-law of Morgan Jones, has written an admirable introduction to Morgan Jones' life and Dylan Rees wrote an outstanding article on Morgan Jones' contribution towards education in *Morgannwg* (Vol. 31, 1987), the Journal of Glamorgan History. Both have provided very useful background information. I have also been fortunate in the fact that correspondence from Morgan Jones has been reproduced in *Llafur – the Journal of the Society for the Study of Welsh Labour History (Vol. 1, 1972 – 1975)*.

The Home Front, July 1914 – May 1915

Audrey Griffiths

This essay is based on contemporary issues of Merthyr Express, a local newspaper for Merthyr Tydfil and its large hinterland.

After the country-wide industrial and civil upheavals in preceding years, July 1914 appeared a more relaxed period and advertisements for day trips and excursions as well as local attractions filled the newspapers. On weekdays, Great Western Railway (GWR) offered local residents bookings to places as diverse as Tenby and Llangollen and on Mondays, trains left for West Country resorts and, by changing at Pontypool Road, Guernsey and Jersey were within reach. Occasionally but regularly, London, Folkestone, Isle of Man, Dublin, Aberdeen "and all points between" featured in GWR timetables. If the preference was road travel, charabancs took the population on days out. For those who chose to stay at home, there were band concerts, flower and horse shows and the welcome headline – "*Nelson Handball Court Back in Action*" after necessary repairs.

Chancellor David Lloyd George, generally criticised for introducing financial reforms attacking the pockets of the rich, was admired and hailed by *Merthyr Express* for being "*this man of the people*".

At the end of July, a black cloud hung over the valleys with the publication of the controversial report on the prosecution of the Manager of Senghenydd Colliery after the deaths of nearly 500 men in 1913 with much critical comment on the meagre fine of £24.

Internationally, there had been "*months of professed friendship and collaborations between the British, German and Russian navies*" but on August 1st, the editorial warned, "*We are in the twinkling of an eye, confronted with the prospect of a war of unparalleled dimensions*".

At 11pm on August 4th, came the official Declaration of War.

The next edition reported "*Armageddon is upon us*". Soon, mobilisation of the Navy, Army and Territorials began "*with support from our colonies*"; reservists, escorted by town bands, left by rail and mobilisation notices calling for volunteers and propaganda posters appeared everywhere. Wales was swept by a tide of support: in Briton Ferry almost every man of eligible age registered and the Tylorstown Silver Band joined en-bloc. "Pals" brigades were being formed throughout the Valleys and town recruiting offices were overwhelmed by the patriotic rush of young men.

There was a general feeling of euphoria – but not in all cases. One local lady, annoyed at the cancellation of an excursion, berated the booking clerk, causing him to reply wearily, "*You had better go and tell the*

Germans, Ma-am, for I have nothing to do with it."

People believed *"it will be over by Christmas"* and rushed to volunteer *"before the fun ended"*. At home, miners worked an extra hour on each shift, the Red Cross accepted volunteers, water supplies were put under armed guard, women set up sewing guilds, relief funds were set up *"for the distressed"* – dependents of those young men who had rushed to volunteer – and dire warnings were issued to merchants if they increased prices.

In Aberbargoed, young women handed out white feathers to men who appeared reluctant to enlist, and those men left were exhorted to take up smoking(!) as the taxes raised would support the war effort. Advertisements targeted women to *"Buy a WB corset TODAY and help YOUR country"* and, what is more, *"Every woman in the valleys can help by insisting that the corsets she buys are BRITISH MADE by BRITISH LABOUR"*. Everyone was singing "Keep the Home Fires Burning", written by Cardiff born Ivor Novello, a very popular actor and composer.

After the Battle of the Marne in September, the newspaper headlined *"The Refugees are coming"*, many to be billeted in valley towns although Bargoed disgruntledly commented that it already had an extreme shortage of accommodation. The British and Belgian governments had an agreement that refugees would be welcomed and the first bewildered Belgians arrived in this area in October.

Despite these national events, the minutiae of local concerns are still recorded. Due to increasing attacks on British ships, food shortages were beginning and *"dig your own"* was a common phrase – not without some dissent. A popular column in the paper was *Rhymney Valley Echoes* and one week, the correspondent reported there were many questions about the distribution of allotments in Hengoed and Gelligaer.

Obviously annoyed, he decided to print some of the *questions "in case anybody else has got something in his head"*. Two examples:

- A man from Ystrad Mynach was allowed to apply for an allotment at Hengoed although anyone from Ystrad Mynach would be able to get one under either Caerphilly or Gelligaer Councils - Ystrad Mynach was partly in both councils, and

- A man living in Monmouthshire but intending to move to Hengoed was allowed to draw for an allotment before actually living in Gelligaer.

There are many more complaints, so obviously, there was territorial concern at home as well as abroad.

In August and September, the Battles of Mons, Aisne and Arne had introduced the concept of trench warfare, and in October and November, the Battle of Ypres led to very heavy casualties on both sides. The horrors of war, and especially the trenches, were described by men coming home on leave, and *Merthyr Express* increasingly reported the deaths and injuries of local men. In December, many casualties resulted from the bombardment from sea of Whitby, Scarborough and Hartlepool.

Mobilisation continued and here is a moving description of "The Departure Platform at Cardiff Station" on Thursday, September 14th, 1914 when the University Principal and his staff were shaking hands with their students:

"Women students, despite a surface gaiety, were betraying signs of strain of farewell. Some were already engaged to men who three months before, had been destined for posts in the professional world. During the next few years, daily trains carried men returning from leave and one woman called that departure platform the valley of the shadow of death."

Christmas was celebrated as traditionally as possible. Tirphil held a party for 250 wives and children of soldiers. Needlework groups were busy making "trench socks" for the military, Rhymney Baptists sent "War presents", and many funds were raised for the wounded, Belgian relief, tobacco for soldiers and comforts for regiments. There were "patriotic" whist drives, dances, tea parties and many, many flag days. Obviously, the soldiers were being given a great deal of support – occasionally, in a strange way. In Maesycwmmer, a men's group which had previously met for political discussions during which arguments were so ferocious that members were nicknamed "The War Office", decided that strife was no longer appropriate. To celebrate a more peaceful union, a presentation was made to a local resident, Lieutenant Seaborne, on leave from the Front.

The coming of 1915 also brought the realisation that the War meant a long commitment. News from the Front was not good and the papers printed longer and longer casualty lists. Theatres now presented plays with war-related themes. Refugees continued to arrive; they were welcomed in Rhymney but Merthyr was asked to accept more. Increasing attacks on the British fleet meant that news about food shortages was occupying more print space. Merthyr butchers appealed to customers to cut back on meat in order to provide for soldiers; local relief committees provided funds for the needy; cookery columns contained recipes for cheap soups and home bread making was encouraged. A local councillor officially complained he had seen the top and bottom crusts of loaves on a scavenger's cart.

Reports of 580 women and 560 waifs and strays admitted to county workhouses caused concern and, noted particularly, was the distress of children with sick mothers and fathers in the army and special criticism was aimed at the custom of sending orphans to workhouses.

The stalemate in the War and the absence of men, except for those in reserved occupations, saw more emphasis given to the role of women. Discussions at Education Committee meetings often concentrated on the employment of women who had previously been forced to resign upon marriage. There were complaints that male teachers *"out of service for 20 years"* were given preference over these well-qualified women. However, discussing the appointment of a woman head teacher at a junior school, a councillor (female) feared that *"a woman would not be able to discipline large boys."*

Early 1915, the propaganda machine for women went into action. The suffragettes, so active pre-1914, halted their demands until the end of the War, but their leader, Mrs Pankhurst, badgered the government to use women to fill the vacancies left by men. To persuade officials and the general population, the paper had a list of *"mechanical devices emanating from the brain of women"* including gloves to turn into mittens for use on the Front, collapsible bedsteads to be carried in knapsacks, paper clothing, supports for mosquito nets etc. Local women who volunteered for foreign service were profiled: Dr Margaret McKillop, Assistant Schools MOH announced her departure; Nurse Smith of Gelligaer Isolation Hospital had returned home after 3 months in Serbia only because the hospital was captured. At a reception in her honour, she announced she had again volunteered her services.

There was concern that while the number of male drunkards was down, the number of females was up. Women received criticism for not taking up the opportunity of attending evening schools. A council member complained about attendees, *"some were even past their prime. It was a waste of money for old people to go and wag their chins."* Advice was handed out to women who *"spent vitality on trifles, fretting away energy in a score of ways without results"* and girls overspending on clothes were admonished if they thought it *"will make it easier to meet a man who will support them in luxury. This is a delusion".*

For some women, times were very hard indeed. As many families shared houses, Caerphilly set aside and furnished three rooms in Castle St. for soldiers and their wives to enjoy a break. But there were reports of cruelty inflicted by soldiers on their families while on leave and also by civilians. In Dowlais, a husband kicked his wife to death in front of their young children. And under "The Battle of Hengoed" was the report of *"a dispute between respectable neighbours, resulting in strangulation, scratching, thumping, tearing of clothes and a woman being thrown into a garden by her hair.*" Luckily, an advertisement had the solution "*to the extra pressure being put upon women over 30, now reaching the age of going downhill.*" Dr. Williams' Pink Pills for Pale People guaranteed success.

May 1915 was especially bad. At home, the miners were dissatisfied with wages being the same as in 1910 even though mine owners had enjoyed a 50% increase in the price of coal since 1914. There was more talk of the dreaded conscription, and Bargoed and Bedlinog established "No Conscription Fellowships". As the military suffered a severe shortage of shells, the much admired Lloyd George was appointed Minister of Munitions. News from abroad was of more casualties and fewer victories, and the first Zeppelin raids on London caused many deaths and injuries.

May 15th brought the shocking news that the SS Lusitania, "a ship of peace", had been sunk by German torpedoes with no warning. 1200 civilians died including 35 out of 39 infants travelling with their mothers to be with their Canadian fathers who had enlisted in the British Army. Eye witness reports were widely printed and, since more than 120 American lives were lost, it was expected that America would now intervene in the conflict, but this did not happen for another two years.

There were some interesting local connections. Deep Duffryn Colliery at Treharris was the sole source of coal for the record-breaking pre-War Atlantic crossings of both the Lusitania and her sister ship, the Mauritania. Aboard the doomed ship were members of the Royal Gwent Welsh Singers whose tenor was from Blaina. Also aboard was D.A. Thomas, an influential coal owner, with his daughter, Margaret Haigh, a determined and active suffragette. Both escaped, and he became of great assistance to the government, rewarded by being made Viscount Rhondda in 1916. After his death in 1918, by special dispensation, Margaret succeeded to his title and became Viscountess Rhondda.

May 1915 was a crisis point and the government felt forced to declare a state of "Total War". This put the whole country on a compulsory war footing with the government in complete control. The next year, conscription was introduced, but it was not until 1918 that an Armistice was signed. In 1938, Lloyd George described the War as "the most concentrated slaughter, mutilation, suffering, devastation and savagery which mankind has ever witnessed".

<u>Just one year later the Second World War began.</u>

Audrey Griffiths ©2013

Bedlinog funeral with full military honours : October 1915

Annie Owen

The harsh reality of war was brought home to the Bedlinog community with the poignant events of early October 1915. Gassed while on active service in France, 30 year old Private Mordecai Williams died in a London hospital Sunday, October 3 1915. His body, having left that hospital on Tuesday, arrived in Bedlinog at 1 am on Wednesday, and was buried with full military honours on Friday, the first event of its kind in Bedlinog.

Hundreds of local men, women and children lined the route as the funeral procession made its way from Bedlinog to Graigfargoed Cemetery. The tragic side of war was evident as the procession, led by a squad of soldiers from Cardiff with reversed arms and a slow step, and Bedlinog Brass Band (enhanced with some of Treharris Band), playing funeral marches, progressed up the hillside, its pretty autumn scenery far removed from the horror of the battlefield. Behind them came Local Relief Committee, St. John Ambulance Brigade, Fire Brigade (under command of Brigade Surgeon Dr Llewellyn), Red Cross Nurses (under Commander Miss Gunter of Trelewis) and R.A.O.B. and other Friendly Societies. Then, his coffin, draped with a Union Jack on which his hat and trumpet had been placed, was followed by family mourners, behind whom were hundreds of men and women. Rev. W. J. Williams of

Photograph of the family gravestone in Graigfargoed Cemetery by Roy Smith

39

Trelewis officiated at the graveside in Graigfargoed Cemetery, where his body was laid to rest in the same grave as his two siblings who had died in infancy in 1890, and his mother who had died 1891. The soldiers fired their volley which echoed in the mountains and the Last Post was played.

Who was Mordecai Williams?

Mordecai Williams was descended from a local farming family, the Williams family of Nantwen. His grandfather, land surveyor David Williams (1822-1859) married London-born schoolmistress, Matilda Brasted (1824-1907) in 1848, and they had a daughter, Elizabeth, and three sons, David, Edmund Phillip and William Henry. After the death of her husband in 1859, widowed Matilda brought up her young family at Nantwen, home of her late husband's unmarried siblings, Thomas (1809-1882) and Margaret (1812-1873). Her three sons were still there at the time of the 1881 census when Matilda was living with Elizabeth, by then schoolmistress at Gwehelog, near Usk.

Matilda's middle son, Edmund Phillip, became a colliery blacksmith, and married Ann Roberts, and their children (including Mordecai, born 1886) were born in Bedlinog. The family, living at 34 High Street when the 1891 census was taken, was saddened by the death of Ann just a few months later. They moved to 4 Station Terrace before the 1901 census. By 1911, Edmund, together with his older surviving daughter and a granddaughter, lived at 8 Station Terrace, while Mordecai (described as a colliery assistant roof repairer) was at 37 High Street in the household of David Edwards and his wife, who was probably sister to Mordecai's late mother, Ann.

What is known of the military career of Mordecai Williams?

Commemorated on both Bedlinog War Memorial and Guest, Keen and Nettlefolds' Bedlinog Colliery Memorial, it is likely that collier Mordecai Williams was working locally when war broke out in 1914. Having enlisted for war service at Merthyr Tydfil, he served, Private 15948, in Royal Welsh Fusiliers 9th Battalion.

Name.	Corps.	Rank.	Regtl. No.
WILLIAMS.	R. W. Fus.	Pte.	159 48.
MORDECAI.	—"—	—"—	—.—

Medal.	Roll.	Page.	Remarks.
VICTORY	J/2/102.B.7	1858	D of W. (GASSED).
BRITISH	— do —	do.	3/10/15
15 STAR	J/2/2/B 3.	477	

Theatre of War first served in // France.
Date of entry therein 19. 7. 15

K. 1280.

His battalion, 9th (service) Battalion, Royal Welsh Fusiliers, was raised at Wrexham September 9 1914 as part of Kitchener's Second New Army and attached to 58th Brigade, 19th (Western) Division. They trained at Tidworth before moving in December 1914 to spend the winter in billets in Basingstoke, and returned to Tidworth in March 1915 for final training before going to France, landing at Boulogne July 19 1915. Their first action was at Piltre, in a diversionary action supporting the Battle of Loos (opening attack of the Battle of Loos). It is not clear exactly when and where Mordecai Williams was gassed or when he arrived in the London hospital where he died.

Sources

Merthyr Express (issues of October 9 and 15 1915).
Buick, Greg *Parish of Gelligaer, The Farms and their Families 1540-1840, volume 1, Garthgynydd Hamlet*, pages 84-86. (2010)
Various websites including
http://www.cwgc.org/find-war-dead/casualty/2759672/Williams,%20Mordecai .
Bedlinog war memorial on www.gelligaerhistoricalsociety.co.uk
World War One memorial plaques produced by Guest, Keen and Nettlefolds to commemorate the men who died in that conflict and worked in Fochriw and Bedlinog Collieries http://www.fochriwhistory.co.uk/page486.htm

Trelewis responds to The Great War
Alun Watkins

It seems incredible that a butterfly flapping its wings in the Amazonian rain forest could ultimately cause a hurricane in another part of the world. But that is a tenet of Chaos Theory which contends that a single occurrence, however small, can lead to large-scale, unpredictable variations in the future. It is even more unbelievable that the assassination of the Archduke Franz Ferdinand and his wife, in the distant Bosnian capital, Sarajevo, on 28th June, 1914, could lead, eventually, to the slaughter of over 9 million combatants world-wide, within the next fifty-two months.

On August 3rd, Bank Holiday Monday, 1914, there were more than 50,000 people, mostly from the mining villages of South Wales, enjoying themselves in the sunshine at Barry Island. Few, if any of them, were aware of how close the country was to war. None of them could have imagined the catastrophic events which were to follow when Great Britain declared war on Germany, the very next day, to protect Belgian neutrality. To think that war would last for 4 years and entail such immense loss of life would have been laughable. But that was to be the grim reality. The *Merthyr Express*, in its editorial for the week following the declaration of war, opened with the prescient words: "The Armageddon is upon us." There had been little mention of such an occurrence in the July editions, but plenty of advertisements for Bank Holiday and summer excursions! From August, 1914, there would be whole pages of war news.

When the outbreak of hostilities became known, it was not long before the villagers of Trelewis began to react. Their response was:

IMMEDIATE

Reservists in the armed forces were called up by the Government to be sent to the front. Within a week of war being declared, the *Merthyr Express* was reporting that 50 reservists from the locality had left on the mid-day train from Nelson and Llancaiach station, for depots in Cardiff, Lichfield, Bodmin, Devonport, Oxford and London. They were given a rapturous send-off by a crowd of several hundreds who cheered them on their way. All were confident of a speedy resolution to the conflict. Horses from the district were also commandeered by Government agents. Thousands upon thousands were required as the horse was still the prime means of moving heavy guns and military equipment in a less mechanised age. They were also needed by cavalry regiments. Some idea of the vast number involved can be found in the estimate that almost half a million horses were killed during the fighting. In the very first week of the war, therefore, some Trelewis farmers and tradesmen had their horses taken from them. The consequences of this have been well-captured in the Michael Morpurgo book, *War Horse*, and in the subsequent film and play. Whether those in Trelewis, who forfeited their animals, considered their sacrifice worthwhile is open to conjecture.

Reservists from the three Welsh regiments (South Wales Borderers, Royal Welsh Fusiliers and the Welsh Regiment) contributed to the six Infantry Divisions which comprised the tiny British Expeditionary Force sent to face the enemy in 1914. The numbers were woefully inadequate. Lord Kitchener, the most distinguished soldier of the day, became Secretary of State for War and realised that many more would be needed. Instead of introducing conscription, he called for volunteers between the ages of 19 and 35 to join his "new army" which he hoped would comprise 70 Divisions. Thus he began an outstandingly successful recruiting campaign, utilising his incredibly powerful poster. His eyes magnetically pin-pointed the passer-by, his outstretched forefinger pointing unmistakeably at him with the message - "Your country needs YOU!" A huge response from volunteers was to follow. While there have been those who have questioned Kitchener's military strategy, no one has impugned his recruiting ability. Mrs Asquith, the Prime Minister's wife, rather unkindly indicated this when she remarked that if Kitchener was not a great man, at least he was a great poster.

The number of men from Trelewis responding to Kitchener's call for volunteers grew from a trickle to a flood. By October, 1914, there were 70 names of those who had enlisted since the outbreak of war prominently displayed on the door of St Mary's Church. The curate, Rev. W. J. Williams, obviously thought that by naming and honouring those prepared to serve their country, others would be encouraged to do likewise. So it was to prove. Kitchener had wanted an initial mobilising of 100,000 men but in the first week of September, 1914, 175,000 had been recruited and by the end of the month, the total had grown to 750,000. Throughout the mining valleys recruiting proceeded apace. It was reported that 80 to 100 men each day were enlisting and by the beginning of November, 1914, 300 miners from the Rhymney Valley had joined the Rhondda Battalion. The same month, Lloyd George persuaded Kitchener to create a new Welsh Division (the 38th). Kitchener had rejected Lloyd George's idea of combining the volunteer battalions into a Welsh army because, in his opinion, an entire Welsh army might be "wild and insubordinate"! Instead, he agreed to a Welsh Division.

Why was there such a great response to Kitchener's volunteer army? The powerful propaganda of his recruiting campaign played a great part in this.

The *Merthyr Express* assisted with 3 consecutive advertisements in a month. In them, psychological pressure was applied to arouse patriotism for being a soldier of the King and for having one's name inscribed on a roll of honour. Employers were similarly encouraged to allow their employees to join up. Many of those who enlisted from Trelewis were employed at the Ocean Colliery, Treharris. They could have claimed exemption because of their employment in an industry needed for the war effort. In their case, before they could enlist, permission from the colliery manager was needed. Very patriotically, the Ocean Colliery owners agreed to pay the travel costs of those who wished to enlist at the Recruiting Office in Merthyr. Employers and employees were rallying to the cause. There were also more mundane reasons which motivated miners. The general opinion was that the war would result in victory within a matter of months and volunteering would take them away, briefly, from the drudgery of the pit to adventure, travel and excitement. All of these attractions, together with more money than they were paid as miners, were powerful incentives. Exaggerated hatred of the Germans was whipped up because of their alleged atrocities in Belgium, This was in evidence locally, as a Belgian Refugee family had settled in Nelson. Other more altruistic volunteers were prompted by extravagant hopes of a better world to be established after the war. With all these inducements, no wonder there were those in Trelewis who were ready and willing "to pack up their troubles in their old kit bag" and leave family and friends. They were mainly expecting a good time and to be home for Christmas.

Men were not the only ones to make an immediate response. In the first week of the war, the *Western Mail* appealed for women to come forward to serve as nurses in the 3rd Western General Base Hospital Territorial Service. It is difficult to discover how many women from Trelewis served as nurses or in other capacities during the war but there were undoubtedly a number of them. (One was Gertie Jenkins of Caiach Terrace who served in the Women's Auxiliary Army Corps.) A more readily visible and immediate involvement of women can be seen in the support they gave to the troops. Before the end of August, 1914, about 30 women were attending a sewing class, led by Mrs Leigh, held weekly at Glynbargoed House, to make items for men in the forces. This was so successful that it continued to meet regularly, with increased numbers participating, producing hundreds of garments for Trelewis soldiers and sailors. The example of these ladies in Trelewis was copied by a similar group in Nelson. The village as a whole united, without delay, to aid its men on active service. In August, 1914, a meeting was held at Trelewis School, chaired by Councillor Jonah Evans, JP, which resulted in the formation of a Relief Committee which raised funds to assist dependents of reservists and territorials. Dr W. W. Leigh was to be its President. Both these men had sons who joined the forces and who were to distinguish themselves in the war. They used their prominent positions in the village to ensure that maximum help for the war effort was forthcoming.

The war had begun and Trelewis was not slow in becoming involved. Men and women involved themselves speedily hoping for an equally speedy victory. It was commendable that such a tiny village was to make a response which was:

SUBSTANTIAL

At the start of October, 1914, the *Merthyr Express* stated that over 90 recruits from a village of just under 1,000 inhabitants had joined the new army. This was a remarkable response and the correspondent, probably swelling with pride, was of the opinion that it would be difficult for any village in Wales, of similar dimensions, to match or beat this record. Within a fortnight, however, there had been a revision to the numbers enlisting, As mentioned earlier, the curate of St. Mary's had written only 70 names of serving soldiers on the church door. This wish to claim the honour of sending the most recruits to the war was seen again in February, 1915, when the *Weekly Dispatch* was offering a granite cross to the village which had most enlisted men, in proportion to their population. Trelewis entered the competition, claiming 130 recruits out of a population of about 1,000. There is no record that it won the prize!

Overall, 10% of the Welsh population (proportionately more than from England, Scotland and Ireland), served in the forces during the war. 100,000 Welshmen joined the army before May, 1915. By November, 1918, 275,000 had fought and 35,000 of them lost their lives. Trelewis, despite its smallness, was to make its own substantial contribution to the war. Over 400 men from Nelson and Trelewis had joined up by May, 1915, averaging one in ten of the population. It was estimated that this was practically one in three of all those eligible to volunteer. Looking at the Trelewis Absent Voters Lists for the 1918 General Election gives a real perspective on those who were serving their country. Every street has those away on active service, some from the same house with many neighbours also absent. In all, there are 138 recorded as being absent. Since the voting qualification was 21 years of age, this by no means indicates the total number who had enlisted, as those under the age of 21 are not included. In addition, the names of those on furlough/rest/recuperation or those invalided out of the services are not listed either. There were certainly considerably more than 138 who had served by 1918.

The youth of those who responded has been well-documented, many getting away with volunteering under-age. One of these was J. N. Nathan of High Street. He enlisted when he was only 15 years of age and spent his 16th birthday in the trenches. He was subsequently discharged for being under age but rejoined the Machine Gun Corps when he became 18. That demonstrates the tenacity of youngsters who would not be deflected from joining in the conflict. Pte. Tom Storey, also of High Street, was another. After being rejected 5 times, such was his determination to enlist, that he underwent an operation in order to become medically fit to join the Coldstream Guards. (Sadly, he was killed in action in September 1916.) There were others too, from Trelewis, who did everything possible to join up to serve their country

Possibly the best indication of the total number who served is given in the letter of apology which Dr Hubert V. Leigh, Glynbargoed House, sent regretting his failure to attend the unveiling of the Trelewis War Memorial in May, 1925. He wrote that "Trelewis had done its bit" in the war, when 375 men had served in His Majesty's Services (Army, Royal Navy, and Royal Flying Corps). This was from a small village of 600 houses. He also pointed out that in that number were several from the village who had emigrated to the colonies and who had served in the Australian, Canadian and South African forces. These included: Lieutenant J. H. Evans, son of Jonah Evans, who was a member of the Australian forces; Private Llewellyn Palmer, serving in the 51st Canadian Infantry and Private Sam Jayne of the South African Infantry. To have so many serving in the forces was a substantial record of which the village could be proud. It would have been a worthy tribute if all the names of the 375 who served in the Great War could have been included in this article but that has not been possible. The names of those mentioned are, therefore, intended to be representative of their comrades. Obviously, this account is by no means comprehensive, and fails to depict the total response made by Trelewis to the Great War. But, hopefully, it provides illuminating, if incomplete, insight into aspects of that response.

In addition to substantial numbers, Trelewis soldiers showed substantial bravery and heroism during their service. To give some examples: In October, 1918, Company Sergeant Major W. T. Owen of St. Mary Street was presented with the Military Medal (M.M.) and Bar at Cardiff Barracks in recognition of gallant conduct in France in 1916 and 1917. The M.M. was won at Loos on December 21st, 1916, when the Welsh Regiment was making a raid on enemy trenches in 3 parties, each under an officer. All the

Officers were wounded and Owen took sole charge, successfully completing the raid. On returning, he picked up an officer who had fallen on the parapet of the German trench and carried him to safety. The Bar to the M.M. was gained at Bourlon Wood on November 21st, 1917. All the Company officers were killed or wounded. Sgt. Maj. Owen again took charge and consolidated the position until relief came on the 25th. His fearlessness and devotion to duty reveal a man of whom the village could be proud.

The same can be said of Sgt. James Northey of the Welsh Regiment, who was a reservist when the war broke out. He went to France with the first draft of the expeditionary force, fighting in the battles of Mons, Aisne, Marne and Neuve Chapelle. When home on leave in the summer of 1915, he married Beatrice Allen of Caiach Terrace. In January, 1916, he was awarded the Distinguished Conduct Medal (D.C.M.) for conspicuous gallantry. He went out over the parapet four times under heavy shell fire and brought in four wounded men. When he came on leave, he received a very warm welcome with the street decorated in his honour. Unfortunately, he was severely wounded in the Battle of the Somme, was transferred to hospital in England but died shortly afterwards, with his wife and mother at his bedside. His D.C.M. was presented to his wife at a presentation made at Trelewis School in April, 1917.

Frank Parry of Penygraig Fargoed Farm was well known in the local farming community, winning several prizes in ploughing competitions before his 17th birthday. He enlisted in the Grenadier Guards at the outbreak of war and transferred to the Welsh Guards on its formation in 1916. His father was to receive a parchment certificate from Lord Harlech, Colonel Commanding the Welsh Guards, recording the gallant service of his son at the battle of Loos in September, 1915. This stated that Private Parry had remained on Hill 70 with 3 other Privates in a hole between the British and German trenches with 2 German prisoners and a dead German officer. They remained there for some days, living on food taken from the Germans, until they were able to return with their prisoners. For this brave action he was promoted, on the field, to the rank of Corporal. He was 21 years old.

These are but three examples of the bravery displayed by Trelewis soldiers which received official recognition. But there were countless other occasions when their fellows showed their mettle on the battlefield, not always resulting in the award of medals or commendation. Their efforts are praiseworthy too. Amongst others who did gain recognition were: Gunner Alfred Stephens, Royal Field Artillery, (Military Medal), Private Sid

Williams, Dorset Regiment, (Military Medal) and Corporal Robert Jenkins, Welsh Regiment, (Military Medal). All deserved the admiration and grateful thanks of Trelewis. That this was readily forthcoming is seen in the way the village feted those returning home on leave during the war. The encouragement and support for those defending their country was nothing less than substantial. Streets were decorated, suppers and concerts were held on numerous occasions. The pages of the *Merthyr Express* record many "smoking concerts" to celebrate the homecoming of those wounded in action or returning on rest leave. The Ffaldcaiach Inn and the Bontnewydd Hotel were the main venues and a large attendance was guaranteed. Chapels, too, welcomed home those of their number on active service. Everything possible was done to encourage those serving their country. Another example of this was wounded soldiers from the Caerphilly Red Cross Hospital being entertained at Glynbargoed House. The village was proud of all those serving their country and wished to show its gratitude in a practical way.

As the war progressed, the early optimism began to subside. By the end of 1914, the war had become a slogging match with combatants bogged down in continuous trench warfare. One Trelewis soldier serving there wrote about the rough time he was having, alleviated a little by news of home. He particularly mentioned the rush to read the *Merthyr Express* which Sidney Evans, the son of Jonah Evans, received from Trelewis each week! But nothing could erase the pain or the hardship of being involved in unremitting, miserable trench warfare. Despite huge loss of life, very little advance was made and the most that was gained, by either side, was a few miles. This was because of the immense power of machine guns which mowed down advancing infantry and made the cavalry utterly useless. The complex systems of heavy gauge barbed wire entanglements also contributed to the stalemate. To cross No Man's Land was a formidable and almost impossible task. Trelewis was to discover that its involvement in the Great War was:

COSTLY

In all, 45 young men from Trelewis died. This number compares with the loss of 13 lives in the Second World War. (Practically every war memorial in the country records how much greater the casualties were in the 1914-18 war.) As the losses mounted, the villagers feared for the safety of their loved ones. The knock at the front door and the arrival of a brown envelope were greeted with ominous foreboding. Every one of those who lost their lives is worthy of commemoration but this account can remember only a few. One of these was Sergeant John Thomas Jenkins, (known as Little

Jack, presumably because of his size), Royal Welsh Fusiliers, the son of Mr and Mrs R. Jenkins of Caiach Terrace, who was killed in action on July 20th, 1916. He was 23 years of age and had been at the front since September, 1915. A popular sportsman and good footballer, he had worked at the Ocean Colliery prior to enlistment at Merthyr. His Commanding Officer, Captain E. M. Sell, wrote to his parents that Jack was one of the best men in his Company and knew no fear. Company Sergeant W. E. Phillips also wrote that Jack was a good friend of his, very popular and one of the best and bravest N.C.O.'s in the battalion. A fellow Sergeant from Trelewis, in the same battalion, Sgt. Harry Price, in a letter home wrote: "One of my chums has been killed - Jack Jenkins. I don't know his people's address or I would write to them. He lived near the Ffald somewhere. I would like you to go to tell them that Little Jack died leading his platoon into action, and setting a good example to the N.C.O.'s under him. We were out for a walk a few nights ago and he was saying there were only three of us from the village in the battalion. Tell his Mam that the little hero died quite peacefully and suffered no pain. Please offer them my sincere sympathy in their sad bereavement."

These were typical of the communications received by the bereaved on the loss of their loved ones. One wonders whether they always told the complete truth. Sgt. Jenkins died at the Battle of Delville Wood and there is strong evidence that many of the Royal Welsh Fusiliers who died in that engagement did so as a result of "blue on blue" fire. The 10th Battalion apparently went astray and came under fire from a British machine gun barrage, losing many as a result. 91 men of the battalion died at Delville Wood, or were missing, with a total of 228 casualties from the engagement. Mistakes happen in the heat of battle but that is no consolation for their families. (So-called "friendly fire" is never friendly to those who suffer from it!) Sgt. Jenkins' younger brother, William, also served in the war, but he survived and returned home to live in impaired health.

Neighbours in Bontnewydd Terrace received fateful news almost at the same time. Mr and Mrs Richard Ninnis of No. 3 were officially informed that their son, Private Willie Ninnis, King's Shropshire Light Infantry, had been killed in France by a German shell, after two years at the front. Shortly afterwards, their neighbour, Mrs Jones of No. 2, whose 3 sons were serving in the army, received a letter from Sister Eva Schofield of No. 2 General Hospital, Le Havre, stating that despite strenuous efforts to save her son, Gunner Bob Jones, Royal Field Artillery, he had died in January, 1917. In October, 1918, Mrs Jones was to receive more devastating news. One of her other sons, Lance Corporal Joseph Jones, Machine Gun Corps, had died of pneumonia in a hospital in Archangel. He had gone to Russia 6 months previously with the N. Russia Expeditionary Force. The sorrow and heartache caused by war was certainly felt in Bontnewydd Terrace.

One feels for parents who had more than one son serving in the forces: they had double the amount of worry and concern for their offspring. This was true of Councillor Jonah Evans. In 1915, it was reported that his eldest son, Sidney, was serving somewhere in France and his second son, James, in the Dardanelles. Similarly Dr and Mrs W. W. Leigh, Glynbargoed House, had two sons serving abroad. They would have been gratified to learn of the commendation of their eldest son, Captain H. V. Leigh, when he was mentioned in despatches during campaigns in Egypt. Originally, Capt. Leigh had been attached to the Welsh Regiment but responded to the urgent call for doctors by transferring to the R.A.M.C. When in France, he was one of the first volunteers to fill the places of fallen doctors. He served there in the trenches for the whole of 9 months fighting before being put in charge of a dressing station and afterwards of a base hospital in France. Subsequently, he was moved back to Egypt where he became Registrar in charge of the 27th General Hospital, Egyptian Expeditionary Force. However, Dr and Mrs Leigh received distressing news about their second son, Lieut. H. G. T. Leigh. He had, before the war, emigrated to South Africa for the sake of his health and had engaged in farming there. In 1915, he joined the South African Artillery and took part in the campaign in German West Africa. Later, in 1917, he returned to England and joined the Officers' Training Corps in Cambridge before gaining a commission in the Labour Corps. After a brief furlough at home, he was sent to France but was only there a short time when he was taken ill and transferred to the 8th Red Cross Hospital at Boulogne. His condition deteriorated and became so serious that his father and mother were sent for. He died on November 11th, 1918, the very day of the Armistice and was buried on November 12th in the British cemetery at Boulogne, with full military honours. Instead of celebration, there was to be sorrow for the Leigh family as peace was proclaimed.

This was to be the case for other families in Trelewis as well. Amongst these were the parents of Private W. H. Lewis, Welsh Regiment, Bontnewydd Terrace. He died of pneumonia at Redcar in December, 1918. There was a short service at the house, conducted by the Rev. W. D. Nicholas and at Beechgrove Cemetery, led by Rev. W. J. Williams, Vicar of Ystrad Mynach. Large numbers attended including members of the Caiach Lodge R.A.O.B. and soldiers on leave and those already discharged. The village joined together in a poignant memorial to those who had got to the end of the war but who did not survive to enjoy the peace. It was a tragic time whenever families received the sad news of the loss of their loved ones and, even more so, when more than one member paid the supreme sacrifice.

Mrs Mansell of Mackintosh Terrace received news that her husband, Private Thomas Mansell, Welsh Guards, had been wounded severely in both legs and died of his injuries in July, 1917. He had worked at Treharris and Penallta collieries before enlisting in the Grenadier Guards in November, 1914. Transferring to the Welsh Guards, he was severely wounded in 1916 which required several months in hospital. On his recovery, he had returned to France to enter the conflict again. Mrs Mansell received a message of sympathy from the King and Queen together with a letter from her husband's Company Officer, Lieut. B. T. Herbert, Welsh Guards. The latter stated that: Private Mansell had been in high spirits with his friends prior to the engagement where he lost his life; he had been a very good soldier and set an excellent example to the younger men both in smartness and in courage. He was only 33 years of age and left a wife and 5 children. His brother, Private Sam Mansell, was a regular soldier in the Grenadier Guards and had been involved in the first engagements of the British Expeditionary Force. He was killed in action a few days before Thomas had enlisted in 1914. The death of his brother did not deter him! Both gave their lives, leaving the Mansell family with a double load of grief.

How sad, too, when one member of the family survived the war but another died. There had been fathers and sons from Trelewis who responded to the call to serve their country. Private Tom Jewell and his son Lieut. W. J. Jewell, South Wales Borderers, of Field Street, were amongst their number. Tom Jewell was discharged from the service in July, 1917, after being wounded. His son, who, prior to joining up, was a miner with his father, had a meteoric rise in the army. He was listed as a Corporal in January, 1916, promoted to Sergeant in May, 1916, and received his commission in September, 1917, before he was 20 years of age, having shown real qualities of leadership. William Jewell was killed in action in September, 1918. The father was not to be re-united with his son at home. War is no respecter of persons or of families.

The cost to Trelewis, of its contribution to the war, was supremely paid by those who sacrificed their lives. But there was also a tremendous cost paid by those who were wounded in action and who came back with physical or mental disabilities, some of which were permanent. For example, Private Dan Jayne of the Shropshire Regiment returned home in September, 1915, to rest after being struck in the right elbow by a bullet. Many men were wounded in the heavy fighting in France that year and, when they returned, the streets were decorated with flags to honour their homecoming on being discharged from hospital. In 1916, Private Fred Thomas of the Welsh Guards lost his right eye and received other wounds in France. The following year, Private C. Blunt, Monmouthshire Regiment, of Bontnewydd Terrace, was severely wounded, receiving injuries to his spine from a bursting shell. Some were discharged from the army as a result of their wounds like Private Fred Brick, Welsh Regiment, of Caiach Terrace, who received an extensive shrapnel wound to his thigh. Also Private Harry Davies, Royal Welsh Fusiliers, of Brynhyfryd Villa, Ffaldcaiach, who was initially wounded at the Battle of Loos but returned to serve in Egypt and Palestine before being severely wounded in the Battle of Gaza, 1917. His shattered arm and damaged hip rendered him unfit for further service. Other Trelewis soldiers returned to civilian life before the war ended, being placed in Class W. These included, Privates T. Batten, W. Bufton, and Driver W. Picken, who left the service in October, 1918. One wonders what the condition was in which they returned particularly if they had been involved in action. Their war was over but others, after recuperating, were returned to their Depot or to the front line. Amongst these were: Pte Lewis Williams of Pontsquire, a reservist in the Grenadier Guards, later of the Welsh Guards; Private W. Hardman, 1st Devons, of High Street; Trooper W. H. Davies, 1st Royal Dragoons, of Richards Terrace.

Appallingly-wounded men were found on all fronts. Some were beyond help; others, whose minds had gone, were beyond communication. The wounded were evacuated to base hospitals and when possible back home e.g. Private Arthur Davies, Welsh Guards, who was returned to hospital here in the hope of recovering from burns sustained in a German liquid fire attack. Military surgeons had to contend with new problems which they had not encountered before such as: "trench foot", recognised by 1916 as a form of near-frostbite; "trench fever" caused by the insanitary conditions and resulting in incapacitating headaches, fever, shooting pains in the shins and discomfort to the eyes. (Private Gilbert Phillips, Gloucestershire Regiment was a victim of the later, in 1917.) Many soldiers were affected by war gases which intensely irritated the eyes and throat, burnt the skin and in some cases killed by asphyxiation. (Hopkin Evans was reported as being badly gassed in May, 1915, one of 181,000 British soldiers gassed during the war.) The horrors of trench warfare also combined to cause a debilitating illness that had not previously been described. Called shell shock by a British physician in 1915, it was only gradually accepted as a psychological condition. Sufferers became hysterical, disorientated, were paralysed or ceased to obey orders and had to be hospitalized away from the front. The cost of the war could be seen in those men who returned. During and after the war, they were found on street corners, in chapels etc. No town or village was without them, some psychologically damaged, some suffering from illnesses contracted during the war, some with disfiguring wounds. They were men literally torn apart - ordinary men suffering with extraordinary wounds. Many never put their lives together after the war. Many did not even wish to talk about what they had experienced. Their handicaps were to be a constant burden to them. By 1930, there were still 30,000 shell shock victims receiving disability pensions.

Amongst others who had to pay a huge cost were relatives who faced the agonising wait for news of those reported missing during the war. This was the case for the families of: Lieut. T. Watkins, High Street, in May, 1915, and Private W. Davies of Warren Terrace, reported missing in September, 1916. Also, Mr Ben Stephens of High Street was notified in October, the same year, that his son David was missing, believed killed. Sometimes there was a better outcome as in the case of Private Charlie Jones, aged 21, the son of Noah Jones, High Street. He had been reported by the War Office as being wounded and missing but in October, 1916, his family received a letter from Pte Jones saying that he was well and a prisoner of war in Germany. While this would provide some relief, there was still the worry of how he would fare as a prisoner. In May, 1918, Private Sam Jayne who had been reported missing was discovered to be a prisoner of war in Germany. Prisoners' conditions varied considerably. Some did agricultural work but most faced inadequate nutrition, miserable sanitary conditions and boredom. 160,999 British soldiers became prisoners of war amongst whom were a number from Trelewis. Regrettably, the outcome for some prisoners of war was not good. Private Jack Williams, Welsh Regiment, had enlisted early in the war and had seen much service, being severely wounded on one occasion before being captured by the Germans. He was the only son of Mr and Mrs John Williams, Glynbargoed Road, who received the news of his death after the armistice had been announced in November, 1918. Hopes of his return were cruelly dashed. It was the *Merthyr Express,* reporting in September, 1918, which captured the prevailing mood of those awaiting news, when it said that "considerable anxiety prevails in the village regarding the safety of many local soldiers of whom nothing had been heard for a long time." The long wait sometimes ended in joy but often in sorrow.

Those who remained in Trelewis during the war years also found how costly world war could be. Early in the war there was price inflation caused, in part, by sheer profiteering. It was a regrettable feature that some tradesmen began charging exorbitant prices for foodstuffs. In an attempt to stop this practice, the *Merthyr Express* took to including a weekly column showing the prices of provisions. Workers complained frequently of the high prices, empty shelves and unfair distribution. Food shortages, brought about by the war, were to cause hardship and, eventually, rationing was introduced by Lord Rhondda when he was appointed Food Controller by the government. Even before that, there were South Wales miners prepared to take industrial action, as early as 1915, to defend their living standards. Restrictions in food were not the only hardships. Clothing, shoes, furniture and other everyday articles were in short supply because of the concentration on the war effort.

The shortage of male personnel, as a result of their absence in the forces, also put added pressure on those who remained. Teachers in particular had responded to the call, leaving schools desperately short of male staff. John Davies, who had retired as Head of Trelewis School in March, 1913, because of ill health, after 31 years of dedicated service, was to have only a temporary respite from his labours. In December, 1914, E. T. Owen, the Headmaster of Nelson Council School enlisted in the Welsh Field Ambulance, R.A.M.C., leaving the school at short notice. Public-spirited by nature, John Davies came out of retirement to fill the gap in Nelson, leading the school until Mr Owen's return in May, 1919. He was prepared to fore-go his own well-being to serve the community, giving Nelson the benefit of his expertise and accumulated experience during the war years. There were some mundane consequences he had to deal with in the school caused by the exigencies of war: staff were instructed to use spaces in old registers in 1917 because of difficulties in procuring new registers; in 1918, only oral examinations could be held because of deficiencies in exam books and other materials. The long arm of war could reach as far as the school.

Women, too, found that war resulted in their following new and different occupations. They did jobs they had never done before, having to replace the men who were away fighting, Women took their jobs as tram drivers, munitions workers, blacksmiths and many other positions in industry and farming. (The *Pontypridd Observer* had advertisements for women tram conductors in 1916.) By 1918, it was estimated that 1.5 million women were employed in jobs previously done by men. The invaluable service they rendered and the abandonment of suffragette tactics during the war, were to be rewarded when women got the right to vote in the Representation of the People Act, 1918, but only for those over the age of 30. Despite hardships there were to be some benefits.

For those who fell, their war was over. But when did it end for their parents, widows, children, relatives and friends? By 1918, practically every household had lost a relative or someone they knew. What was the cost to the millions of men wounded on active service, including those from Trelewis? For some, pensions helped compensate for injury and they eventually recovered. For others e.g. victims of shell shock, little could be done. Millions of widows and orphans produced by the war received some help from the public authorities but no one pretended this made up for their loss. When you think of the broken lives, broken marriages, lost careers and opportunities, then you realise that the war lasted much longer than the four years of conflict. Its cost was incalculable: it was a war which reached out to practically everyone.

Such was the impact made by the war that it inevitably ensured that for survivors and for generations to come, it would be:

MEMORABLE

The rejoicing when the war ended rang through the village. Fog signals and detonators were let off on the railway; engine drivers competed with each other to make as much noise as possible to proclaim the good news; the Ocean Colliery hooter joined in the rejoicing; the solemn tone of the Church bell announced the return of peace. Speedily the village was bedecked with flags. People gathered excitedly and smilingly to celebrate. A general holiday followed the next day and shops were closed. Relief, gratitude, joy, together with myriad feelings of thankfulness united the villagers.

That the war was to be memorable for pupils at Trelewis School can be seen in the School Log Book. In October, 1914, HMI W. Edwards, in his report, wrote that the children took a keen interest in the progress of the war. At St. David's Day celebrations in the school during the war years, there is mention of activities such as recounting the heroic deeds of Welsh Regiments at the front. In the 1916 St. David's Day programme, the school's roll of honour was read out. The pupils were then given the solemn task of making a laurel wreath in memory of the fallen heroes from the village. There were 4 names to be commemorated at this stage: Lieutenant T. Watkins; Sergeant R. Watkins; Corporal. G. Watkins and Private Hopkin Isaac. More names were to follow in succeeding years. Pupils were also made aware, by changes in staff, of those who responded to the call to serve their country. In December, 1914, Mr J. C. Williams left for war service. Thankfully, he was to return and resumed his duties there in June, 1919. Some pupils, anxious to leave school, had cause to be grateful to the war. They were able to claim War Exemption Leaving when over the age of 13. The Head Teacher recorded, rather morosely, that this made them "very indifferent to their attendance". The pupils were pleased, the staff were not.

Some parents in Trelewis made sure that their offspring would find the Great War indelibly memorable. They bestowed on them Christian names which were for ever associated with that conflict such as: "Ypres" and "Dardanelles." Their peers, possibly finding those names difficult to pronounce, took to calling them "Ippy" and "Dardy". How the boys felt about having such names is difficult to determine but they were to be a constant reminder of the war to all who met them. We may think this was unwise of their parents who should have chosen more usual names and is a relic of a past generation. But, in our own time, the practice of burdening children with striking names which find resonance with their parents has continued. Parents have named their children after film and pop stars. Some have gone so far as to give them all the names of their favourite football team! In Trelewis, Ypres and Dardanelles were names which kept the memories of battles alive for another generation.

Shortly after the end of the war in 1918, the Caiach Lodge of the Royal and Ancient Order of Buffaloes had started a movement to erect a war memorial in the village. But when the villagers learned that the memorial was intended only for members of the Lodge, they wanted something more inclusive for all to be remembered. In September, 1919, a meeting was held in the vestry of Ebenezer Chapel to discuss how to proceed and various fund-raising activities began. It took some time for the requisite amount to be raised and it was only when the Trelewis Ex-Servicemen's Club (which became part of the British Legion after it was founded in 1921) was involved, that real progress was made. Previously the Club had been active in supporting the families of those killed and wounded in the war. In all, it took over six and a half years and the overcoming of many obstacles, before an estimable memorial could be constructed on land donated by Daniel Lewis of Bontnewydd Farm.

May 31st, 1925, was an unforgettable day in Trelewis. That was when the Trelewis War Memorial to the 45 young men who had sacrificed their lives in the Great War was unveiled. The whole village turned out for the occasion together with many others from the neighbourhood. A large procession through the village, led by the Treharris Workmen's Silver Band, passed a dense crowd of spectators lining the road, to the site of the imposing war memorial, adjacent to Captain's Hill, where 3,000 gathered to witness the unveiling. A life-size figure of a mourning soldier, made of Sicilian white marble, with head reverently bowed and hands resting on an upturned rifle was the beautiful, even awe-inspiring, recognition by the village of the debt it owed to these gallant men. Two of the youngest being commemorated were only 19 years of age, while the oldest was 46. John Davies, the former Head Teacher of Trelewis School, where most of those being remembered had been pupils, was given the honour of unveiling the tribute. In a moving speech, he recalled how, at school, they had concentrated on learning to prepare themselves for the battle of ordinary life. But, facing an excruciating, costly, and literal battle, they had given their all. As a result, some of them had been interred in foreign soil while others, with no known grave, were simply remembered by name and nothing more. He congratulated the ex-servicemen present on their safe return, paying tribute to those who displayed their medals and to those whose scars and disfigurements gave evidence of their suffering. Looking to the future, he  wished them well. He concluded with a powerful appeal for all to maintain the monument to be worthy of their fallen heroes and to seek an end to war by supporting the work of the League of Nations and the propagation of the Gospel.

The dedication of the memorial followed. Everyone there was moved and much affected by the solemnity and significance of what they had witnessed. Trelewis had wanted to give a worthy accolade to those who had given so much. The beautifully impressive memorial did just that in its simple but nonetheless eloquent inscription on its grey granite pillar:

Erected by the inhabitants of Trelewis
To the Glory of God and the Immortal Memory of
The men of this village who died for their country
In the Great War 1914-1918
They died that we might live
Gwell Angau Na Chwilydd

The response of Trelewis to the Great War was fittingly and powerfully remembered in its War Memorial. But would that memory of those who gave their lives really be immortal? Towards the end of the twentieth century, the War Memorial had become neglected and even vandalised. The words of John Davies at the unveiling, when he expressed the hope that the memorial would be well-preserved and be worthy of pilgrimage, had been forgotten. The British Legion, inspired by its women members, led by Shirley Bufton, was determined to do something about what had become a deplorable situation. They worked tirelessly to raise funds and support to relocate the memorial to a more prominent and safer spot in the village. On June 23rd, 2003, their efforts were rewarded when the memorial was rededicated, after being moved to a conspicuous position, opposite the main road, near the Ffald bridge. There was a procession of about 300 ex-servicemen who marched from the Millennium Park, behind the Salvation Army band, to join the crowd at the newly-sited War Memorial for an Act of Remembrance. Despite the passage of well over 70 years, the names of those inscribed on the village memorial were not going to be forgotten. Age was not going to weary them: they were still to be remembered. John Davies' words were to be appropriately realised in a new generation. In 1925, he had said: "What comfort and consolation have we to offer, if the names of the brave boys, reared, nourished and loyal to the village and country, are not transmitted down to posterity?"

The 375 men who served their village and country so well still deserve to be remembered with gratitude. It is appropriate that, a century later, an article like this should pay tribute to them. Trelewis made a noble response to the Great War which is indeed memorable. The recollection of the hideous slaughter, bloodshed, tragedy and loss should have been sufficient to ensure that nothing like it would ever happen again. After all the horror and suffering, Lloyd George's words to Parliament on November 11th, 1918, were seemingly prophetic: "I hope we may say that thus, this fateful morning, came to an end all wars." But the shock waves of the Great War were to be felt long after the Armistice of November, 1918, and its outcome was to prepare the way inexorably, for another, even more terrible conflict. G. W. F. Hegel's contention that the only thing people can learn from history is that people never learn from history, was sadly to gain some credence, twenty-one years later. The villagers of Trelewis were once more drawn into the painful consequences of a world war, for the second time.

SOURCES AND ACKNOWLEDGEMENTS

Merthyr Express - files for 1914-1918 have been the main source
K. O. Morgan *Wales 1880 - 1980* Oxford 1982
J. Paxman *Great Britain's Great War* London 2013
A. J. P. Taylor *English History 1914 - 1945* Oxford 1965
Alun Watkins *A Village Headmaster - John Davies (1851 - 1942)* Gelligaer 2013
J. Winter and B. Baggett *1914-1918* London 1996

Thanks are also due to the following:
Greg Buick, Webmaster of Gelligaer Historical Society
Richard Evans and his website: www.nelson-ww1-memorial.org.uk
Janet Hughes for her help and advice
Steve Kings and staff of Bargoed Library
Janet Tolley for information on Robert and William Jenkins

Army Service
Glyn Williams
(reproduced by kind permission of his son Dr E.D.G. Williams)

I was called up on April 3rd 1917, & proceeded to Cardiff, via Bargoed, for the purpose of joining up.

In Cardiff Recruiting Office I remained all day until 5.30 pm. at night, when I was given a pass to convey me to Woolwich where I was to join the Army Ordnance Corps, which was stationed at Red Barracks. I returned home that night, & proceeded to Woolwich next day, Wednesday the 4th of April, arriving at the Barracks about six in the evening.

I remained there on Thursday and until after dinner on Good Friday. We had nothing to do only draw a knife, fork, spoon and towel and parade now and again under a typical army Sergeant, who tried to put the wind up us and prepare us gently for army life.

Snow was falling on the ground at 2 o'clock on the Friday when Cpl Edwards (Llanelly) marched us out of Woolwich Barracks, en route for Chatham via Dartford, where we arrived safely after tea. One can imagine my feelings on going from Woolwich and Chatham when I saw miles and miles of flat country stretching out on all sides with parts of the Thames in view in the distance. It was a vivid contrast with the hills and valleys of Wales to which I was so accustomed.

Captain S. M. Noble met us and made a little speech, in which he was sorry we could not be accommodated in billets, but we would be made as comfortable as possible under canvas, (r-r-r-r-r), and were allowed 5 blankets each for the first night.

We got up alright on Saturday morning, only a few chaps were cramped with the cold of the night and Deacon (Cardiff) fainted in the mess room.

After breakfast we paraded and then proceeded to the Casualty Hospital where we were inoculated against typhoid, (T.A.B.7-4-17)

On the Tuesday we were given our khaki clothes and on the Wednesday we again went to the hospital where we were vaccinated (11-4-17). Then again on the Monday (16-4-17) we had the second dose of inoculation and two days excused, as it made one feverish and unfit for work.

By this time I had been put to work in the "Blanket Store" and things went on uneventfully until the 1st day of May '17 when I was picked out for draft for Egypt, and proceeded home for five days leave on the 2nd May.

After a fine time at home I had to return back and leaving home by the 7pm train on Monday 7th I caught the London train at Cardiff at 10.35 and arrived Paddington 3.30 am in the morning.

Then I went to Victoria in a motor and left there for Chatham where I arrived at 6.30 am on the 8th May 1917.

On the same day we were issued with Egyptian equipment, and fully expected leaving at any time. Photos taken on the 13th and received on the 15th outside our tent (number 24) of Wilkinson (London) Gardner (Nottingham) Deacon (Cardiff) Hall (Ashton under Lyne) and myself *[In the front with the hat]*. The other chap Fellowes (London) was out at the time it was taken.

I attended the Central Hall Wesleyan Church every Sunday. The text on the 15-4-17 was John XIV.20 and on the 13-5-17 it was "The door is shut" and a powerful address on that text was given by Rev. H. Whitehead.

We are expecting to go away any day, but nothing comes, and we carry on as before.

I sent my wristlet watch home on 15-5-17 and a watch was sent to me in a parcel on Friday 18th May 17 but I never received it (some one's luck).

The week we returned from draft leave a draft was picked for Salonika and left Chatham for Aldershot on 19-5-17 but our draft still remained.

On 24th I was in the naval dockyard and saw the big naval guns there.

Johnny, Kitty and Jerry were sold at the Waun Fair[2] on Monday May 21st 1917.

Deacon went on leave that week and we still remained.

21st May 1917 was Whitsun Monday. We had the day off and Cpl Hides (afterwards R.G.A.) Holms, Deacon, Hall and myself went for the afternoon to Upnor, which is across the Medway from Chatham and we had a pleasant time. On the same day Fellows went to Sandwich near Dover, and Wilkinson and Gardner went to Plymouth for duty with about eight others.

The garrison baths were now open to us on Thursday mornings at 6.30-7.30 am and it was a treat.

On Monday June 4th was the King's birthday and we had another holiday. In the morning Jim Frost, Claude Evans, Edwards and myself went on the river at Rochester for 2 hours. After dinner we went to the baths again and in the evening for another row on the river with Hall and Deacon.

That evening I saw the first sea plane near the river bank on a platform and that evening it flew up the river and came down it like a motor boat. On the same day we saw a huge airship patrolling over Chatham.

On Tuesday 5th May another Egyptian draft is formed and this also leaves for Aldershot, on returning from leave.

Things go on as usual until Friday June 15 1917 when we have a kit inspection (draft) in the Gun Wharf.

On Saturday we get half a day off to wash our clothes etc. and on Sunday morning we go up for medical inspection and receive pay books.

After dinner we are free, but after tea we again parade, march to camp and are confined to camp for the night (an order broken by many).

---

[2] Horse Fair held each year on Common to north of Fochriw, Gelligaer.

On Monday June 18th 1917 we leave Chatham by the 8.17 train via Waterloo for Southampton. The train went to the quay side and we went aboard S.S. Antrim about 5 o'clock. We set sail about 7.30 pm - 8 pm and arrived at Le Havre about 4 am next morning but did not land 'til 8. The journey across the Channel was in a fog and sirens were blowing periodically through the night.

Three troop ships and two destroyers came across together from England. It was at Le Havre I saw the first German prisoners working with the R.E.'s or Ordnance.

On landing we marched to the rest camp at Le Havre and had breakfast about 10.30 am. We had dinner a few hours later and tea a few hours after that and left to march to Le Havre railway station at 3.30 pm.

About 8.20 pm the train leaves the station and we see some glorious scenery and take a nice joy ride though we are in cattle trucks. The scenery we pass through is glorious through olive plantation and vineyards. The country is all cultivated and there is very little barren land. Fences and hedges are scarce, and cattle are tied in the fields. It was glorious going through France but the French were nearly all in mourning and were very quiet.

We passed through Ju Visi, Dijon, Orange, Lyons etc. and arrived at Marseilles at 8 pm on Thursday June 21st 1917. Then we had a march of some miles to a rest camp and finally went to rest at 12.30 on the floor with two very dirty blankets.

On Friday we managed to get a little breakfast and at 11.30 we were sent to the dock to work (without dinner which we had at 3.30 pm). Similarly we worked at docks on Saturday and Sunday amid figs and raisins.

On Monday and Tuesday we had a rest (June 25th & 26th) and fortunately for us there were shower baths there and we made good use of them too.

On Tuesday I drew a pass to go out to town from 2 'til 8 pm, but (my luck) all passes were cancelled and everyone was confined to camp.

On Wednesday June 27 1917 we paraded at 9 am in drill coats and trousers and marched to the docks, where we went aboard the "Kinfauns Castle". That night I slept in a hammock for the first time and it was all right.

We were still in dock on Thursday and two mine sweepers (Snapdragon and another) lay in behind us. On Friday we were still in dock and two destroyers (Nemesis and Cameleon) came in and lay by our side until Sunday. On Sunday morning July 1st 1917 (4.30-6 am) we commenced our voyage. That afternoon a soldier's body was seen to float past and in the evening two porpoises were seen following the ship. We also had services aboard from 6 pm -7 pm.

On Monday we were not allowed to wear boots but on Thursday that rule was cancelled, as the deck was too hot.

On Friday July 6th 1917 we saw the white walls of Alexandria about 1 pm, landed about 5 pm and went to Gabbari camp.

Our voyage had been an uneventful one. We sighted African coast on Sunday night and took a zig-zag course all the way. On passing Malta on Wednesday morning July 4th we changed our escorts.

We were given Work to do at Gabbari of a light nature commencing on Sunday July 5th. That afternoon I was in town and also Monday Tuesday and Wednesday evenings. Saw many sights including Waza (native quarter). On Monday our clothes, and We were fumigated at Mesc (sic).

On Thursday July 12th we paraded at 4.45 pm and marched to Gabbari station en route for Kantara. We started about 6 pm, slept on the floor of the carriage and arrived at Kantara on Friday morn and saw a glorious sunrise.

We remained there that day and cleaned a little of the mess room and had a bathe in the Suez that evening. At 8.28 on Saturday morning 15 of us proceeded to the station and went to Ismailia and 15 others came in the afternoon. It is here we are to be stationed, the nicest spot in Egypt.

That afternoon I was put to work as a clerk in D Group Harness and Saddlery and do OK under Staff Sergt Owen (Hartlepool).

It's a fine place and we are able to bathe in Lake Timsah adjoining the Suez Canal. This lake is supposed to be the end of the Red Sea in Biblical times and here Moses is supposed to have crossed when taking the Israelites from captivity.

On Thursday July 19th and most subsequent Thursday evenings I went to a Bible class, held at the Egyptian General Mission (Mr & Mrs King's house) under Rev. Wood-all. The subject was Abram's travels through this land from Mesopotamia, mention being made of the corn stores of the ancients at Pelusium and Romani

We heard Lord Radstock speak at the YMCA, on his way up the line.

On Friday July 20th George Taylor (Porth) had a bed but about midnight he and Thomson had to get up and put it out as the bugs were too many for them and bit them.

On Saturday July 21st General visits our depot and we draw pay (the first after Le Havre). On Sunday a service is held in camp and the subject is "Chivalry" by Wood-all. On Wednesday July 25th I received my first letter in Egypt from Saunders.

At the Bible class we are told we are on the borders of the "Land of Goshen".

In Egypt stars are plainer and more numerous than in England and the Milky Way is easily discernable. On Thursday August 2nd we see four Japanese destroyers and a cruiser in Lake Timsah on the way to the Mediterranean Sea.

On Bank Holiday Monday August 6th We get a half day and we play a practise game of cricket. H.M.S. Euryalus is in the canal now. On Thursday August 30th a troop ship Saxon goes through the canal en route for Mesopotamia. I wonder if Jarvis Jones is on it.

On Sunday September 16th I go to Port Said with Kershaw (Leeds) and have a good day. See the canal entrance and monument of M de Lesseps[3] halfway along the pier. He is pointing a finger along the canal and underneath is a Latin inscription and some huge keys, which indicate the opening of the canal. Wednesday September 19th there are aquatic sports down the town. Ordnance Polo Team came second, the ASC Motor Boats being first.

Football season now commences and we beat in succession "Ladybird" (4-l) Eupheus (4-1?) Wireless (9-1) 75 Wab (?) (5-1).

Jack Nutley now goes to Kaun Ynis.

Orders now come that depot is to be closed on October 15th. However it finally ends by issues finishing on that date and we wind up by end of month. The soil around Ismailia is all sand. And only a sea is lacking to make it a sea side resort. Trees line the road from Ferry Post to the town. Palms are abundant also date trees. The weather very hot in summer, very little rain.

On Thursday October 4th Taylor leaves for Sheelal and Thomson for Gamli with them also goes Goodacre, Trowell, Capewell and Phylis.

Shortly We will all be leaving Ferry Post and so on Sunday evening October 7th we had a smoker in the canteen out of accumulated canteen funds.

On Monday October 22nd 4 chaps including Jackson and Hills went to Cairo for duty and we thought "Lucky beggars".

On Saturday October 27th a party of about 35, including myself and Massey, left Ferry Post for opening a depot "somewhere" up the line. We remained at Kantara that Saturday night, and while there I saw Farthing, Trim, H. Albert, Emson and several old boys from Chatham.

---

[3] Ferdinand de Lesseps "built" the Suez Canal.

On Sunday morning at 6.30 we left Kantara and arrive at Rafa that night about 9.30

On the way we passed Pelusium, Romani Dir-Abl, and El-Arish (Where Major Southey was buried). At El-Arish we saw the lightning flashes around Gaza way, and occasionally a peal of thunder.

We remained at Rafa 'til Wednesday doing very little, but on that day the party left for Karm (5 miles beyond the Wadi Ghuzzi) leaving myself with 4 others at Rafa for a week (Ben Stone, Paulin, Patterson Bob Tolson and myself).

During the week at Rafa we watched Gyppos stacking bales of blankets in store tents, and picking up back-sheesh of the R.O.O dump.

On Sunday November 4th we all get aboard a truck, with all our kit etc. in the morning and get breakfast on a siding.

That evening I went from my truck onto another (of mattresses) to convoy three trucks to Karm. In the night I awoke, train was going full speed, and I thought I'd be at Karm by morning. Next morning, however, I awoke and found myself still in the siding as also were the other four chaps. About midday Monday just as we were preparing for dinner, an engine shunts in and takes two of my trucks and leaving the third behind. I rush after Lieut. Belsham who in turn rushes after the R.I.O. and finally I have to run with my kit onto the main line and jump on one of the trucks which is going, leaving the truck of mattresses behind at Rafa.

I soon reach Shellal and afterwards Imara, where I see Harrison, who tells me all about the place. At 3 pm I arrive at Karm which is simply a heap of dust with a lot of tents pitched all around. It was five, however, before I got into the Ordnance Depot owing to shunting operations. Then I handed the charge of trucks over to Sgt. Hallam and had tea after handing convoy notes over to Sgt. Major Ilang (Monmouth.)

On Tuesday Sgt Major told me to remain, and he also tried to get me to stop at Karm but of no avail and on Wednesday I returned to Imara where I found my pals had already arrived although Paulin had proceeded to Karm.

At Rafa on Monday October 29th I saw first enemy aeroplane and have a good view of anti aircraft markmanship. She had been to El Arish, and had dropped bombs but did no damage of a serious nature.

When on convoy at Karm (Tuesday November 6th) I saw a caterpillar in some captured Turkish guns and leave them on Ordnance Dump. Also on the Monday night and Tuesday I could see the shells bursting on the neighbouring hills, and plainly hear the roar of the guns.

I may also mention that while at Rafa, I saw a large number of prisoners in a compound (Germans among them) and they did look a dirty dilapidated lot with rotten boots and torn clothes.

On the Wednesday (November 7th) I was at Karm and I saw about 400 prisoners brought in from Beersheba, and there was one solitary woman prisoner, who fell down and kissed the feet of the Officer in charge of the guard, in order to get away from Turks, but of no avail.

Wednesday afternoon (Nov 7th) I return to Imara (3 miles) and help the others in doing nothing and we did it well.

Glyn Williams (left) in Palestine with two fellow soldiers.

On Saturday 10th Harrison goes to Karm, S/Comdr Clarke having gone there the day previous and now we are left Ben Stone (in charge) Iolson, Jock Paterson, myself and four Arm S/Sergts who are nothing to do with us. WE only had a small dump to receive hospital stores from 35 and 75 C.C.S.'s, but our stay was of short duration.

On Wednesday Nov. 14th Ben Stone, Iolson and myself had to proceed to Karm and although we started first thing in the morning it was dark before we arrived at our destination 3 miles away. We sleep in Payment Issues' tent and here I meet Taylor and old Jack Nutley who is on 28 Shop and Charlton on 52 Shop. We soon settle down to work (myself in D group) but we are only there a short while when we hear that the Depot is to close.

Karm is only the name given by the military and is between Gaza and Beersheba. It merely consists of canteens and camps and a terrible amount of dust which fills every corner. It will also be remembered by us for its variety of centipedes and scorpions, which were everywhere. As Gaza had fallen about this time arrangements are altered and we have to change our residence again.

Our next depot is to be at Deir Seneid, and arrangements are made for a train to leave every evening (4 trains) and the first to leave on Friday November 30th 1917.

At this time I was nearly put in Dock with Diarrhoea, but managed to leave on Sunday evening December 2nd (incident Mule in truck R.T.O. makes us get him out and we tie him to telegraph pole)

We arrive at Rafa during the night and we are put into the hospital siding where we remain for most of the next day. A little before dinner everything is peaceful and quiet, when suddenly up flares one of the tents in flames and we have a warm half hour putting out fires, otherwise it wouldn't take much to burn down the whole hospital.

That afternoon we set off again and after passing through Khan Ynis, Deir el Belah, and Gaza we arrive Deir Seneid next morning Tuesday December 4th.

The party that arrived at Deir Seneid on December 2nd were machine gunned by Johnny who came over in an aeroplane, so we were fortunate although no one was hurt of the A.O.C.

I started work in R & I. with Cooper and Bob Iolson and remain there for a week or so. Then on Dec 16th I started again in D group.

On Dec 17th, 18th and 19th men not previously classified and nearly all were made A1.

On Sunday Dec 23rd Col Fuller leaves us and Col De Smidt takes charge of the depot. The latter came from Salonika and proves himself a sport and a gentleman.

On Dec 25rd 1917 I spend my first Christmas day away from home, in the army and in Palestine. On this day we worked from 10 am til 12.30 pm and have our Xmas dinner at 4.30 pm.

It was raining heavily on Dec 24th and also spasmodically on the 25th, but many found means of drowning their sorrows by getting wet inside as well as out. It was awful to walk about owing to the state of the ground, but thanks to Lieut. Chitham (from Salonika) we had a good dinner of Chicken, Beef and Pudding. Then in the evening Jock and I went to the YMCA and we almost had to swim it as the place was almost under water. On Dec 30th volunteers for the R.F.C. are called for and about 40 apply.

On the same day (Sunday) as Bill Rothenbaugh, Toogood and myself go for a walk we see a number of our chaps around a native place and we see a boy of about 10 with his left hand in pulp and his fingers hanging off his right hand. He must have picked up a bomb and pulled out the pin, or something of a similar nature. He was sent to E.L.C. Hospital. At this time there are rumours of "A" men being put in the Infantry, and numbers put in for the R.F.C. in preference, but few were chosen. We now learn that we are going to close down at Deir Seneid and are opening a new depot at Ludd. On Wednesday Feb 12th there was a great football match between the undefeated Ordnance (Deir Seneid) and the ½ Loyal North Lancs, who were only defeated once, and that at Alexandria. Undoubtedly this was the finest game of football I had witnessed. On opening the visitors broke off on two or three occasions and had hard lines from scoring. Then we woke up and started playing football and also started scoring, as is shewn by the fact that we were leading 3-0 at one time. Then the score became 3-2 and afterwards 4-2 so that we felt quite safe in the assurance of victory for our men. Suddenly in the last 10 mins of the game the visitors woke up and their centre forward (Davies, Chelsea) scored 3 goals in succession, the last being just as the whistle was being blown. Thus we were beaten 5-4 in a most sensational game and there was no ill-feeling or grumbling after it. Everyone was satisfied and went away happy which is more than can be said for many matches in old England.

That evening the visitors gave us a concert with their crack party "The Defaulters" which was great depicting Old Bill and the finest Bint impersonation[4] I had seen up to that time.

We are now going to close down at Deir Seneid owing to unsuitability of position and our next Depot is to be at Ludd.

On Feb 20th S/Comdr Purser Allan and Arthur Gould and myself leave for Ludd, to receive stores from Kantara. (It was at this time I learn that Evan Davies is at Ismailia). We leave Deir Seneid at 9.30pm and Arrive at Ludd on Friday morning 21st Feb 1918. As we have nothing to do we have a look round on Friday and get caught in a shower of rain. On Saturday we start work as Camel gear and P.S.G.S. sets arrive.

On Monday I have the afternoon off and go to Ramleh which is about half an hours walk from Ludd. First of all we get some wine in our water bottles and then we visit the market and afterwards we enter the grave yard of the R.C. Church where the Hon. Neil Primrose P.C.M.C. was buried. It is a very simple grave with a plain cross at the head and the following inscription: - "In memory of Capt. the Hon. Neil Primrose P.C.M.C. killed

---

[4] Female impersonation.

in action November 15th 1917" (Bucks Yeomanry) (Son of Lord Rosebery and son-in-law of Lord Derby.)

The R.C. Church is a nice building with a clock tower. On the entrance gates is the following:- "Hospitium Nicodemi Arimatheae". We now pay a visit to the tower (The Martyrs Tower) where 40 martyrs were said to have been imprisoned. It is a fine ruin and about as high as a pit stack. We climbed on the top and looked around but did not remain long you can bet. Near it are the remains of the third oldest church in the world.

A beautiful view of Ramleh and neighbourhood is received from the top of the tower. There is a grave yard nearby which looks very picturesque from above. Graves are all covered with a little building and we saw some native women kneeling near some of them. Evidently they were mourning the loss of a loved one, but were not too much overcome to prevent them asking for "backsheesh"

There are underground vaults near the ruins of the old church which appear to be the (crypts?).

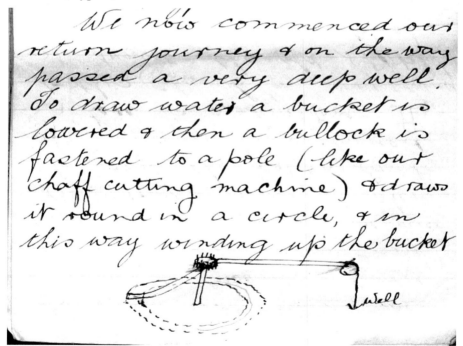

On the next evening we wandered towards Ludd village. They also have a well here and here we saw St. George's Church where St. George the patron saint of England was buried. There is a high tower to this church and every evening at sunset the old Sheikh (Priest) goes on the top of this tower and cries out some prayer.

During the week ending March 16th and previous week I was with S.Q.M.S. Owen issuing to first line transport. Then I returned to group and had a pretty busy time.

On March 26th 1918 a draft of 40 "A men" left Ordnance for the Infantry.

On Good Friday we were all sat down at lunch when the fire alarm went and we all had to run down to the depot. When we got there we found Provision Office (2 tents) burnt to the ground. No more smoking in the Depot after that although Officers still carried on as they were put outside Depot.

On Sunday April 14th I report to Transit at 4 pm and leave on convoy for Jerusalem. I leave Ludd that evening and arrive at Artuf early next morning. Here my stores were transferred to narrow gauge railway and it is near Artuf on top of the mountain is to be seen "Samson's tomb." After Samson raised the Gates at Gaza it is said he returned to his native place Artuf and died there.

I remained at Jerusalem 'til Friday, leaving at 10.15 am and arrived at Ludd about 3 pm on April 19th Friday.

Things run along smoothly until 3rd May 1918 when we get a concert by a party of 21st Corps Details called the "Meteors". It was a fine concert and while it was on old Sid Pembroke and Cockney came in drunk and sat in the officers' chairs and pulled out a bottle. Of course they were immediately evicted and no sooner than they got out when rifle shots were heard. We thought they were up to mischief; but we soon discovered that the S.Q.M.S. stores were on fire and nearly everyone was drunk. Yates got a stray bullet in the head but was only grazed and was soon out of hospital. Old Lawrence and 2 others got 21 days for being implicated in the fire and old Wadams made a fool of himself in his speeches during that time.

Things again went on swimmingly and we got a concert party from the Leicester Rgt. (7 Ind Division) called "The Black Diamonds". This was by far the best party we ever had and they remained 3 nights. On the last night they gave us "Dr Faust" and it was great. Their bint was the best ever heard, voice and everything perfect.

Brogan is gone to GHQ and I am made L/Cpl.

Then comes news of a Coy. being formed to go to India and nearly all our camp volunteer (at least all the NCO's except one, Phillips) and one or so privates.

Finally it developed and matured and on 2/7/18, after having 2 days holiday we left Ludd about 8 o'clock at night.

Then we had a fine ride over the desert and landed at Kantara on Sunday 21st July about dinner time. We remained there a week (too much) and for a few days I worked in D Group on the Dump. I managed a bath in the canal nearly every day and had quite a good time, meeting Deacon, Farthing etc. besides, Charlie Price, Fred Liddle, Bill Bridges, Hibbert etc. etc.

On 24th July I visited Ismailia to see Evan Davies, but learnt, to my regret, that he had left a few days previous for Shalufa near Suez (10 miles).

Then on 1st August we left Kantara about 8 pm and arrived Suez the same night. We had a long march to the rest camp there but were fairly comfortable in no time and made ourselves cushy for the night, although it was a little cold.

Early next morning (about 4) we were awakened by a lot of buzzing and discovered that we were next to an aerodrome and this continued each morning.

On August 3rd we left the Rest Camp and boarded the "SS Nile" leaving Suez next day 4th August for Bombay.

We arrive Aden on 7th and then Bombay on 13th after being sea sick and feeling rotten.

Our party now split up into 3 sections and ours went to Colaba Camp and remained there 5 days before leaving for Karachi.

In the mean time we had a good look round Bombay including Grant Street and were very pleased with what we saw.

On Sunday August 18th We left Bombay on the mail boat "Linga" and arrived Karachi on 20th after a very rough passage. Again we had a day in a rest camp and saw Karachi including Zoological Gardens.

On 21st August we left for Quetta by train. We were put 10 in a carriage, with a fan each, ice-chest and Chatties[5] of water. After a fine journey, rather hot, over the Sindh Desert, and nice through the hills after leaving Sibi we arrived Quetta August 22nd at about 4 pm. This was on a Thursday and next morning we went for a medical inspection and then went to the Arsenal for particulars to be taken.

On Saturday we were allotted to our various groups for duty and on Monday we started work. I was put in Group IV F and G (Guns and Parts) but did nothing 'til the Thursday when I was detailed for duty at the DADOS 4 (Q) Divn Office which was at Divisional Headquarters.

---

[5] A porous earthen pot used in India for cooling water.

Work was quite decent but we had to work Saturday afternoons and our Conductor was not up to much, - tried to get us working Sundays and overtime.

The Arsenal got holidays on Monday 6th September and on 13th September and the following Thursday owing to native festivals. We on DADOS staff got half a day when Bulgaria gave in and considered ourselves very lucky.

By this time six of our men were at Juzzak GPC under Lieut. Chester and later Pte. Wenman joined them.

Evidently I thought I'd have a holiday so I reported sick on November 6 and got put in hospital with a slight touch of Influenza. During the month previous this epidemic had been rampant and it is said that 80 valuable lives were lost in one month.

However I was not bad and was only in a week coming out on Wednesday November 13th. I suppose, seeing that peace was declared on the 11th inst the doctor thought he had better keep me in until the canteens were sold out and then I'd be safe.

The Arsenal was closed on Thursday and Friday November 14th and 15th and on the former day a march past of the troops took place on the racecourse.

On Monday November 18th I commenced Work at the Arsenal as our branch of DADOS staff was transferred to the Arsenal for convenience.

On Saturday the 16th 15 AOC men are expected from Meerut (having been invalided from Mesopotamia) and they were to be housed temporarily with Massey and myself. Rations were drawn and preparations were made but they did not turn up. Therefore we had a good feed and this continued for over a Week until the rations were stopped.

In April 1917 Glyn Williams was 19 years old, youngest son of Thomas and Margaret Williams, Graig Rhymney Farm, Tirphil. He had attended Lewis School Pengam from age of 11. After his army career he went to Aberystwyth University. He studied history, not mathematics, at which he was very good, because of the break in his education. He taught in Gilfach Boys Junior School and the Senior School and Technical School in Bargoed before becoming headmaster of Bargoed Boys Junior School in 1948.

France

Jan 13th 1917

Dear Brother

Just a line hoping that you are
in health the same as I be at
present. Sorry that I have been
so long before writing but
better late than none at all
you can see by the letter that I
have shifted been here a month
now Christmas dinner in the trench
I am sending this letter on
spec because I do not know
if I got your right address
My address is Pte D Williams 61935
11 Pantoon 19 Welsh Reg C. Coy
B E F France
Mind to put all that on the
letter and then I will have it
I had a letter from home to day
and they said that there is a

a month since they had a letter
from you have you seen any
chap that you knows there
yet I have seen a couple out
here, you wait till the war
is over and we get back
home then we will have
a time and that won't be long
I hursting this will find you
in the best of health
from your truly Brother
Dai
send back soon

A letter written to Glyn Williams, who was in Alexandria, by his elder brother Dai, from the trenches in France, in January 1918 (Dai has done what many of us do in January and forgotten that the year has changed – hence the 1917).

Dai never got to "have a time" when the war ended. He was killed in action March 23rd 1918 and was buried at Gommecourt British Cemetery No 2, Hebuterne in the Pas de Calais region of Northern France. He is commemorated on the Tirphil War Memorial.

Photo of Dai's grave in France (2012) courtesy of Glyn's great grandson Macsen.

In the footsteps of Heroes
Six Brithdir Volunteers and the 16th (Cardiff City) Battalion
Royston Smith

After the War Office sanctioned formation of a separate Welsh Army in November 1914, a vigorous recruitment campaign began across Cardiff and District to raise the required 1000 men. Although the campaign was largely restricted to the Cardiff area, many recruits joined from other parts of South Wales, so it was by no means an exclusively "Cardiff" battalion. Among the volunteers who answered the call for this new Welsh battalion were eight colliery workers and residents of Brithdir: William Davies, Harry West, Arthur and Charles Gardener, David John Williams, Harry Harris, Stephen Williams and Ernest Dallimore.

Born in the coal and iron town of Blaenavon in 1880, **William Davies** was son of iron miner Thomas and his wife Ann. On the death of his father, in 1892, twelve year old William became the family's breadwinner, supporting himself, his widowed mother and three younger siblings. Sometime after, the family moved to Brithdir and made their home at 10 James Street. William joined the Territorial Army and his service in the South African Campaign earned him both the Queen's South African Medal and the King's South African Medal. At the outbreak of the First World War, he rejoined the colours. Enlisting at Bargoed in November 1914, he joined the newly-formed Cardiff City Battalion of the Welsh Regiment and was appointed to 'D' Company as Private 24302.

Harry West, born in 1894, was the second of seven sons of Harry and Elizabeth West. He and his siblings grew up in Clapham Terrace, amongst the tightly packed rows of iron workers' cottages in the small village of Forge Side, on the hillside to the west of Blaenavon. When, in 1907, his father accepted the pastorate of Beulah English Baptist Chapel, the family relocated to Brithdir, and took up residence in Treferig House in Church Street. Harry junior, then aged 13, and his elder brother Arthur found employment in Elliot's colliery.

Pastor Harry West Snr.

About the same time as Harry was settling in Brithdir, another newcomer, young Gertrude Cresswell, moved into James Street with her parents Edwin and Emily. Gertrude became Harry's wife December 20 1913 and with their daughter, Mair Elizabeth, (born in 1914) they settled into family life at 9 Station Terrace.

Life for Harry, Gertrude and Mair Elizabeth, changed when twenty-one year old Harry West attested at Bargoed December 31, 1914. He enlisted into the Welsh Regiment and joined Cardiff City Battalion as Private 23795. It must have been a bittersweet moment for him to return home from the Recruitment Office, kiss his wife and infant daughter goodbye, before, on January 1 1915, leaving to join his unit at Colwyn Bay.

Brothers **Charles** and **Arthur Gardener,** natives of Worcestershire, moved to Brithdir post 1911 in search of work in the local coal industry. The brothers, both single, were lodging at 3 Tennyson Terrace when they enlisted at Bargoed on January 8 1915 and were duly appointed Private 23777 and Private 23764 respectively. Both named their mother Margaret of Dudley Road, Lye, Worcestershire, as next of kin.

Bedlinog born **David John Williams** aka 'Dai Brithdir' came to the village at a young age and, when the 1901 census was taken, he was a 14 year old coal hewer, living with his grandparents at 5 Station Terrace. He married Lily Coombs of 7 Charles Street in 1906 and they made their home three doors away from her parental home at number 10. They had three children, Winifred born in 1907, David in 1908 and Aulbrey, born in the June of that long hot summer of 1914 while Europe was preparing for war. Aulbrey was just an infant when his father, enlisted in Bargoed on January 18 1915 as Private 24051 and set off to join his unit in Colwyn Bay the following day.

Son of an Isle of Wight mariner, **Ernest George Dallimore,** his wife, Alice Emily Maud, and two young children, moved to 13 Tennyson Terrace sometime after the 1911 census was taken. Their third child, Ivor Thomas Dallimore, was just two weeks old when Ernest George Dallimore (a colliery timberman) joined the Regiment and, as Private 24440, was posted to join the battalion at Colwyn Bay on February 26 1915.

Harry Harris, born in 1885 in Wood Lane, Stalbridge, North Dorset, was

Cardiff City Battalion under training on the North Wales coast 1915
by kind permission of Celia Green.

one of eleven children of Joseph Harris, an agricultural labourer, and his wife Jane. His route to Brithdir was via Aberaman (Cynon Valley) where he worked as a coal miner and met widow, Lucy Hannah Lewis, who he married at Bethany Congregational Chapel, Aberaman, January 15 1910. Sometime after 1911 the couple relocated to Brithdir. Harry enlisted at Bargoed on March 1 1915 and, as Private 24482, departed for Colwyn Bay the next day leaving behind his heavily pregnant wife Lucy and three children at 2 Tennyson Terrace.

The service records for **Stephen Williams** have not survived. However, his memorial scroll reveals he was a resident of Brithdir who enlisted in Bargoed and joined the 16th Welsh as Private 23221.

The 16th (Cardiff City) Battalion was formed at Porthcawl, but in December 1914 moved from there to Colwyn Bay as part of 130th Brigade, 43rd Division. The next eight months were spent in North Wales, before moving to Winchester in August 1915 with other units of the 38th (Welsh) Division. Quartered at Hazeley Down Camp, they commenced a period of Musketry Training on the Lark Hill and Bulford Ranges. By November, the 38th Division was considered ready for active service, and was inspected by Her Majesty Queen Mary on Salisbury Plain.

The Cardiff City Battalion marching through Cardiff, which included a parade at the Arms Park, before the battalion left by train for Southampton from where they sailed to France on December 4. The line of soldiers stretching into the distance represents a total of 1,025 brave men, comprising 30 officers and 995 other ranks, everyone a volunteer.

Used by permission of Michael Jones, Millbank Primary School, Cardiff.
Image donated for the schools centenary and Remembrance Day display, copyright unknown.

After the inspection, the whole battalion left by train for an emotional final visit to Cardiff, where, on arrival, they were given a rousing reception by relatives and friends. After the usual ceremonial march past, the men had 24 hours leave before returning to Winchester to await the final movement order for France.

To France:

The weather was very wet when the battalion, comprising 30 officers and 995 other ranks, left camp at 6.00 am December 4 1915 and marched to Southampton, where, at 2.00 pm, they embarked for France. In his personal diary (reproduced on Fact Sheet 6-E03-13 in Regimental Museum, Brecon) Private Link wrote of the voyage to France:

"We marched in Full Kit to Southhampton Docks and embarked on the SS Marqarette – a Paddle Steamer. We were packed like Sardines, and after dark sailed for France. It was a very rough night, and nine out of ten, were ill. We got to Le Havre at 7 am on Sunday."

After safely disembarking in France, the battalion assembled and marched

77

to No 5 Rest Camp where they remained until 6.00 pm before taking the train at Gare des Marchandises and departing Le Havre at 9.10 pm. When the train arrived at Aire Sur Lys at 6.30 the following morning, the battalion continued the journey by marching to St. Quentin where it went into billets in farms and farm buildings. On December 20 they marched from St. Quentin, leaving at 8.30 pm and arriving at Robecq at 2.15 pm.

The battalion left Robecq on December 29 in military buses and proceeded to Vielle Chapelle before marching to St. Vaast where they joined the 58th Brigade for instruction. Following a period of trench instruction in the Line with the Guards Division, the battalion took over a section of the trenches in the Moated Grange Sector, near Neuve Chapelle. From then until the following June, the battalion gained considerable experience of raiding and trench warfare as they held, in turn, various sections of the line from Givenchy to Laventie. On June 11 1916 the City Battalion together with other units of the 38th Division withdrew from the Line, moved into billets at Robecq, and prepared to move south to the Somme for the great Offensive of July 1916.

The buses used were London 'B' type buses, some 1,300 of which were requistioned by the Army in October 1914 as troop-carriers on the Western Front.

To the Somme:

On June 14 the battalion marched eleven miles to Auchel where they spent the night in billets before journeying twelve miles the next day and moving into billets at Monchy Breton where they remained for ten days training.

Following a strict Brigade training programme, whole days were taken up with daily marches, physical drill, rifle drill, and bayonet fighting. After inspection of arms, equipment and billets in the late afternoon of June 26, the battalion marched nineteen miles under cover of darkness via the small farming villages of Ternas, Buneville, Houvin Houvigneul, Ligny-Sur-Canche and Vacquerie-le-Boucq to Fortel. They had a brief rest before marching eleven miles through the night of June 27/28 via Barly and Outrebois to Autheux, where on June 28, **Private Harry West** was posted to 15th Battalion. On June 30, they marched fifteen miles to Toutencourt where they billeted in hutments (wooden huts used by the military as temporary accommodation). After a few days rest, they marched twenty miles, arriving at Acheux at mid-night on July 2 and bedded down under canvas. They moved to Buire-sur-l'Ancre on July 4 and again rested under canvas. Following an inspection of arms, equipment, gas-helmets and goggles, they marched the final leg to Carnoy on July 5. In the evening of July 6 the battalion proceeded cautiously to take a position in front of Mametz Wood where they sheltered out of sight of the enemy behind a slope in the landscape.

Mametz:

The 16th (Cardiff City) Battalion experienced major losses in the Battle for Mametz Wood especially on July 7 1916 when the battalion came under heavy machine gun fire from Flatrion Copse and Sabot Copse and they were forced back. They made two more attacks but position was much too exposed for any hope of success and orders were received to cease operations. Battalion Losses: *"6 Officers killed, 6 wounded, 268 Other Ranks killed, missing and wounded."*

Private **William Davies,** aged 37, was one of the thirty killed July 7 1916 and laid to rest in Flatiron Copse Cemetery. The only comfort for his loved ones back home was the knowledge that he had a grave, unlike over three times that number lost that day with no known grave and commemorated only on the

Flatiron Copse Cemetery, Plot X, Row E, Grave 7.
The inscription reads: 24302 PRIVATE W. DAVIES WELCH REGIMENT 7TH JULY 1916
Courtesy www.BritishWarGraves.co.uk

Memorial to the missing at Thiepval.

His commanding officer, Eddie Williams, sent a beautifully decorated condolence scroll to the family which reads:

"It is with feelings of deepest regret I have to inform you of the Death of Private W. Davies. My Platoon, which formed the front line of the attack on Mametz Wood, was practically wiped out. The men followed me gallantly, and it was cruel to see them before the hail of bullets. They gave their lives cheerfully for the dear Homeland and the folks at home."

Private 23221 Stephen Williams, wounded and hospitalised in Rouen, died July 17 1916 and was buried in St. Sever Cemetery, Rouen. As he was in hospital in Rouen it is likely that he was wounded in the Mametz operations either when the Welsh took a hammering during the initial assault on Mametz Wood on July 7, or on July 12 when the battalion suffered further losses due to enemy shelling (after which the 38th Division was moved away) – he would have had to be found then removed via a Field Ambulance and Casualty Clearing Station then slowly transported to Rouen, where he died.

Private 24051 David John Williams had been in France just three months when, in March 1916, whilst in the trenches at Festubert he suffered inflammation of his right eye and it is recorded on his casualty sheet that he had *'trouble with conjuctivitus on and off ever since'*. Appointed Lance Corporal on March 23 1916, he was with his battalion at the hell that was Mametz.

Although costly, the battalion, together with other units of the Division had in five days of extremely hard fighting succeeded in clearing the Germans from the greater part of the wood. It was so badly mauled one of their number later said 'the Cardiff City Battalion died on the Somme' though in reality, they continued to serve until 1918. After Mametz, the Division spent some time in the Courcelles sector until in August 1916 they were moved up to Ypres to take over trenches in the North Western part of the Salient. On the 20th, the 16th Welsh relieved the 1st King's Own Regiment in the line. A quiet period followed with working parties detailed on repairing and clearing trenches. Throughout September, October and November, the battalion took its turn in several locations namely Lancashire Farm, Turco Farm, Canal Bank, Ypres Asylum and Chateau des Trois Tours.

After eleven months service in France, Private Williams was posted back to the UK and reported to the Welsh Regiment Depot on November 25 1916. On February 16 1917 he was deemed more valuable to the country in civil

In 1966, David John Williams and his wife Lily celebrated their Diamond Wedding Anniversary.

Photograph courtesy of their granddaughter, Miss Lily Williams.

rather than military employment and, posted to Army Reserve Class 'W', he was sent back to his former job at Powell Duffryn's Colliery in New Tredegar. In Class 'W', while he was not allowed to wear uniform, he was liable for recall to the colours. However, May 31 a Medical Board at Cardiff, deeming his disability to be the result of exposure whilst on active service, recommended his transfer to Class 'P' of the Army Reserve.

Finally discharged from the army on August 25 1918 with a pension of £21, David John Williams returned to Brithdir and lived in Charles Street for the remainder of his life.

Harry West's War:

Harry landed in France with the main body of the 16th Battalion and, while at the Infantry Base Depot for the Welsh Regiment, he was 'volunteered' for the newly-formed Trench Mortar Battery. Almost immediately on December 23 he was posted to the Trench Mortar Battery (TMB) and sent for training at 1st Army School of Mortars. On January 6 he left the School and it seems likely he returned to his original brigade alongside his pals in 16th Battalion as no transfer is indicated. He remained in the TMB

Private 23795 Harry West wearing the Cardiff City Battalion badge on both collars.

until he was placed sick, although it does appear he was quite ill. On December 30 1916 he was admitted to 34 Field Ambulance with Pyrexia (fever) of Unknown Origin; moved up the chain to 46 Casualty Clearing Station where he was diagnosed with influenza before moving to 2nd Australian General Hospital in Wimereux, France from where he was transferred back to the UK on January 20 1917 with Trench Fever. On leaving hospital he was attached to 3rd Battalion on light/training duties, probably to allow him to regain full fitness before re-joining his unit overseas.

After his recovery Harry returned to the BEF, embarking at Southampton on June 11 1917 he landed at Rouen on June 12th and was initially posted to 10th Battalion, before being posted to 15th Battalion. On July 27 the battalion had taken up positions in the front line in the Zwaanhof sector,

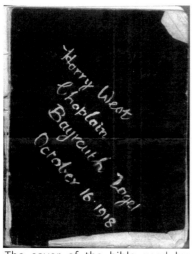

two platoons from the 15th Welsh were sent out to check the German positions, the patrols were met with strong opposition and were forced to hurriedly withdraw. The Germans retaliated by hitting the front line trenches with an artillery barrage, mixing up some gas shells into the bombardment for good effect, and the battalion suffered heavy casualties as a result. The war diary showing figures of three officers and twenty-one other ranks killed, three officers and sixty-one other ranks wounded, and a further thirteen men missing.[6] One of the missing was Pte Harry West and, July 28 1917, he was reported as a Prisoner of War. He was repatriated and discharged from the army April 12 1919.

The cover of the bible used by Harry West as Chaplain in the POW camp at Bayreuth.

Harry returned to Brithdir and mining and, like his father before him, he became a Baptist lay preacher. As the Minister of Brithdir Beulah Baptist Chapel he was invited to Brithdir School Girls Department on Remembrance Day 1919 and an entry in the school log written in the hand of head teacher Miss Mary John, records his visit:-

"Today is Armistice Day. His Majesty's Message has been read to the assembled girls and we have all united in a reverent remembrance of the Glorious Dead paying them a tribute of Silence for a brief space of two

---

[6] Steven John, Carmarthen Pals, A History of the 15th Welsh Battalion, page 117

minutes. Mr West, who was in France as a Chaplain twelve months today gave the top class girls a short address".

Later, Harry West entered politics. In 1925 he was Liberal candidate for a  constituency in the Forest of Dean. He changed to support the Conservative Party, working at Conservative Central Office in Cardiff and, fighting two General Elections only to be defeated in 1950 (by Clement Davies in Montgomery) and in 1951 (by Jim Callaghan in Cardiff South East). He continued to work at the Conservative Office and held the position of Director of Public Economy, keeping watch on the spending of money by Glamorgan Council. Harry West died in 1957.

Photographs and details of his life were kindly given by his daughter Olga courtesy of Mrs Jacqueline Tiernan (daughter of Olga's cousin).

In 1901, seventeen year old **Harry Harris** was a boy soldier with the Royal Scots Fusiliers at Maryhill Barracks in Glasgow. Sources studied to date have not shed light on that early part of his military career but his WW1 discharge papers show that, by December 1915, when he landed in France with the 16th Welsh, he had been promoted to the rank of Corporal. Having served just 59 days with the BEF, a gunshot wound to his right knee meant he was posted back to the UK January 31 1916. He was transferred to the 3rd Welsh Depot before, as a result of a misdemeanour whilst Corporal of the Hay Guard, he was demoted to Private. When he was discharged from the army on August 29 1916, his address was 13 School Street, Tirphil.

Private 23764 Arthur Gardener was nineteen when he landed in France with the 16th Welsh December 4 1915 and he remained with the BEF in France until September 1918. Transferred to the 15th Welsh in May 1918, he was wounded in action by a bullet to his left forearm and posted back to the UK. Admitted to a military hospital September 20 1918, he remained there for thirty-three days before being transferred to Paddington Military Hospital for a further seventeen days. Due to a 40% disability he was awarded a weekly pension of eleven shillings and discharged February 3 1919. Married during 1918, on leaving the army he took his wife, Elsie Louise, nee Edgecomb, to his native Worcestershire where they lived with his widowed mother at 82 Dudley Road, Lye.

Pte 23777 Charles John Gardener married Alice Stinton of Wollaston just two and a half weeks before he embarked for France where he served a total of three years and thirteen days with the BEF. The army was reorganised in early 1918 and, on February 27 1918, the 16th Welsh was disbanded with troops transferring to other units. Charles was compulsorily transferred to the Machine Gun Corps and given the new number 166059. They were in action on The Somme, in the Battles of the Hindenburg Line and the Final Advance in Picardy. On January 19 1919 he was transferred to Class Z Reserves and discharged. At first, he returned to his native Worcestershire before taking wife Alice and baby John (born in 1916) back to south Wales.

Private 24440 Ernest George Dallimore had already served 7¼ years in the Royal Marine Artillery prior to joining the 16th Welsh. With such experience under his belt, by the time he embarked for France nine months later he gained rapid promotion through the ranks to Lance Sergeant. His service with the BEF lasted just 95 days. In March 1916 he was admitted to Third London General Hospital in Wandsworth suffering Acute Nephritis; He remained there for thirty three days before being transferred to Paddington Military Hospital for a further seventeen days. No longer fit

for war service, he was discharged from the army on July 5 1916 and returned to Rhymney Valley, living for some time at 24 Pritchards Terrace, Phillipstown.

Three of these Brithdir heroes received the **Silver War Badge and Certificate**, issued in the UK to service personnel who had been honourably discharged due to wounds or sickness during WW1. Although the badge was not a high level award, in recognising those who had spilled their blood for their country, it was still a significant one.

Regt No	Rank	Name	Badge No	Cause
24051	L/Cpl	Williams David J.	243,611	Sickness
24440	L/Sgt	Dallimore Ernest G.	504447	392 (xv1) KR
24482	Pte	Harris Harry	420,574	392 (xv1) KR

Note: 392 (xv1) under Kings Regulations; cause of discharge - No longer physically fit for war service.

It was the practice of some women to present white feathers to apparently able-bodied young men who were not wearing the King's uniform. On June 13 1918, one year five months and two weeks after his discharge,

Harry Harris wrote to the army requesting his badge as he was often stopped and asked why he was not wearing it. Two weeks later his badge and certificate was issued.

The Welsh Dragon memorial at Mametz Wood

A magnificient Red Dragon monument to the Welsh Division at Mametz is the most striking memorial I have seen. Standing atop a granite plinth and clutching strands of barbed wire in its claws, the dragon glares in defiance facing Mametz Wood where William Davies – and so many of his comrades – fell.

I visited the site with Morgan, my twelve-year old French grandson, and, as we walked across the fields towards Mametz Wood, my thoughts turned to the words of survivor Albert Evans of Cardiff, quoted in Ivor Wynne Jones' Sacrifice at the Somme. Aged 91, Albert Evans made the pilgrimage for the unveiling of the monument in 1987. Having been brought down by a bullet in his right leg he recalled:

"Men were falling everywhere. It was terrible. I crawled for about half-a-mile and took shelter in a shell hole, where I remained for three days, surrounded by the dead and the dying."

I could only image the hell those brave Welsh souls had faced, yet as we walked in the footsteps of heroes, I felt forever proud and honoured to be Welsh.

Authors Note on sources:

- *Personal details about the soldiers are based on research using Army Service Records, War Diaries, Medal Index Cards, War Badge Roll, census returns and their family's personal memorabilia.*
- *The main source for details of the battalion in France was the war diary for the 16th Battalion, The Welsh Regiment, held by the Regimental Museum of The Royal Welsh at Brecon Barracks. My utmost gratitude goes to Celia Green, Customer Services Manager, who lent her expertise and shared information from the regiments' archives.*

Farming 1913-1919

Notes on some purchases and out-goings of the Lewis family at
Clwydtrawscae Farm during the Great War

Judith Jones

These notes have been made from receipts and invoices which have survived for the period of the first World War for Clwydtrawscae, a small upland farm near Bedlinog. The entire extant bundle of receipts and invoices, dated between the 1870s and 1930s, is in very poor condition, many items broken and completely illegible, so they cannot be said to illustrate the complete picture of the income and expenditure of the family at any time. They do, however, give a hint of household and farm expenses, of what the family bought for themselves and the farm, of the shops and companies where they bought items (the invoice headings in italics below) and of how much they paid.

The main out-going each year was the rent to the Pontypool Park Estate. In the Agrarian History of England and Wales, Joan Thirsk wrote . . . *summary of fragmented evidence about the level of agricultural rents in the five years before 1914 suggests an average of between £1 and £1 5s per acre . . . from 1s per acre for hill grazings in Wales and Lancashire . . .* and she also estimated a 6% increase by the end of the War. In light of this, therefore, Clwydtrawscae rent seems reasonable. It was approximately 11s 4d per acre, an annual rent of £35 15s which remained constant throughout the period; during which occupiers, Ann Lewis and thereafter her son Thomas, were invoiced half yearly on the traditional days of 2nd February and 2nd August. The family appears to have been consistently late with their payments however, the February rent invariably being paid in May each year.

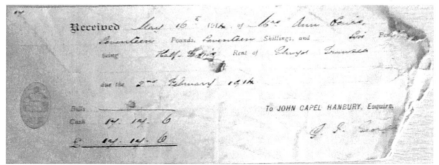

The half year rent of £17 17 6 on Clwyd Trawscae due 2nd February 1914 was paid May 16th 1914.

The General and Poor Rates were another regular expenditure, based on the rateable value of the land, £21 and the buildings, £6.

Parish and Urban District of Gelligaer	Poor Rate			General District Rate			Annual total		
1913	£5	12s	9d	£2	0s	4d	£7	13s	1d
1914	£5	4s	6d	£2	2s	3d	£7	6s	9d
1915	£5	1s	9d	£1	10s	4d	£6	12s	1d
1916	£4	19s	0d	£2	2s	2d	£7	1s	2d
1917	£5	17s	6d	£2	0s	9d	£7	18s	3d
1918	£6	17s	9d	£1	14s	8d	£8	12s	5d
1919	£8	6s	9d	£3	8s	3d	£11	15s	0d

The annual amounts paid for the General Rate fluctuated through the war years while those for the Poor Rate, although showing a decline until 1917, rose considerably during the last years of the war. By 1919, both rates showed an increase of approximately 50% on the pre-war payments.

Household expenditure covered a number of items. The family bought coal in half ton loads from *Williams and Jones, New Gelligaer Colliery*, from *Wern Ganol Colliery, Nelson* and from *Pencaedrain Farm Colliery, Bargoed* (£1 per ton throughout the period). Between January 1915 and January 1916 Thomas Lewis paid nearly £2 to *T. Thomas M. R. Ph. S., chemist of Treharris* – although, unfortunately there is no record of his purchases. In 1914 the family were buying most of their groceries from *J M Rees of Bedlinog*, but subsequently they went to *T. Llewelyn, Fochriw* or to *Sidney Phillips, Pentwyn Stores* (previously *George and Sons*), buying mainly butter, rice, bacon, tea, onions and on just two occasions, sugar, as well as oil (for lamps). They also patronised Fochriw butchers, for example, in October and December 1916, when they bought beef and pork from *John Matthews* there. By 1918 they had returned to buying their "goods" from Bedlinog, and in addition to their usual purchases as above, they also bought matches, Brasso, Lux, candles, polish and black lead. It would appear that they purchased few luxuries – although they regularly bought drinks for the summer months; casks of cider from *Charles Thomas & Sons, Fruit Growers and pure cider makers of Canon Pyon, Herefordshire,* which were delivered to either Bargoed or Bedlinog Railway Station and cider and perry from *Joseph M. Parry & Sons, Leominster*, delivered to Fochriw Station, paying 7d per gallon for cider and 10d for perry; both cost 2s for carriage with an 8s deposit on the cask.

Clothes were a considerable expenditure. For example, in February 1913 Thomas Lewis paid 12s for a dark brown corduroy jacket, purchased from

Mrs Lewis Davies, tailor and draper of Plas y Coed, Bedlinog, estd 1875, and in September of the same year his mother paid £3 3s for a new "fancy suit" from *J. C. Evans, ladies and gents tailor, Llwynon, 10, Capel St., Bargoed.* In November 1916 Thomas ordered a man's suit (£3 3s) from *Capital and Labour Clothing Stores, 59 & 61 Queen St. Cardiff* (perhaps for his marriage in December). On 11th January 1916 the Lewises bought a pair of mens (14s 6d) and ladies (8s 11d) nailed boots from *W. Lewis, Boot and Shoe Merchant, Oakford House, Fochriw.*

The company names on the farm invoices also make interesting reading, particularly the advertising of the extensive products for sale, such as those sold by William Lewis & Sons of Pontypridd described below.

In April 1913 Thomas Lewis bought 10 tons of manure (2s 6d per ton) from Nantwen Pit, the invoice payable to the farm owners, *GKN (successors to Guest & Co. the Dowlais Iron Company, the Patent Nut and Bolt Company Ltd and Nettlefords Ltd).* This may have been waste from the pit ponies or it may refer to slag, waste from the GKN Dowlais Steel works a commonly used fertiliser. He was a customer of *William Lewis &*

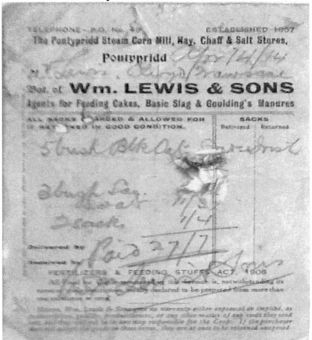

Sons, The Pontypridd Steam Corn Mill, established 1857, hay, chaff, straw, corn, flour, seed, salt and potato merchants, agents for feeding cakes, cattle and calf spice, basic slag, Goulding's manures, Vaporite, cattle oils and agricultural implements, reeds and thatching spares, buying, for example, 5 bushels of barley oats (15s) and 2 bushels of seed oats (11s 3d) and paying 1s 4d deposit on two sacks in April 1914; 9 bushels of barley (£2 11s 9d) in May 1915 (sent on the Taff Vale Railway to Nelson station)

and a sack of winter wheat (£1 9s 4d) in February 1917. Thomas Lewis also bought mixed feed from *W. P. Edwards of Gilfach Farm, Bargoed* (13s 6d per lb), and every May bought root seed, such as "swede, the World's Best" (3lb for 5s 9d) from *Toogood and Son of Southampton (seedsmen to H. M. the King and to H. M. the late King Edward and for 50 years to H. M. the late Queen Victoria)*.

Repairs to machinery and tools were a constant expense, with bills relating to a saddle (15s) (undecipherable company name) and to a chaffing machine (14s 6d) to *Evan Morgan Jenkins & Co., Implement Agents, plumbers and tinsmiths, dealers in timber, bricks, cement and sand and all building requisites. Estd. 30 years, Brecon and Merthyr Railway Wharf, 30, Union St. and Horse St. Dowlais)*. They also bought tools. In August 1918, for example, Thomas bought a rake (1s 8d), a file (7d), a pick handle (1s 6d) and 4 gate hinges (4s 6d) from *E. Harding, wheelwright, coach builder, shoeing and general smith and implement agent, premises at the corner of Capel Street and South Street, Bargoed*. This company constantly repaired the farm's milk float, Thomas paying a total of £6 13s 5d for six repairs between December 1914 and June 1918. The float was important however, because Thomas sold milk daily in Bedlinog, selling far more than he could produce and buying extra from "Squire" Jenkin Edwards of Bedlinog Farm. For this extra milk he paid an average of 10d per gallon, and receipts for the period show that he bought between 115 and 135 gallons per fortnight.

Medicines were bought for the animals, mainly from *Noah Rees & Sons of Cardiff* and in 1916 they paid 4s 3d for sheep dip to *Osmond & Son, wholesale chemist and druggists, animal medicine and cattle food specialists, sheep dip & disinfectant manufacturers* of Grimsby (the farm continuing to purchase medicines from both companies until at least the 1970s) and 3s to *Bristol Veterinary Medicine Co. Ltd., St. Paul St., Bristol* in October 1915.

In July 1914, 1915 and 1916 Thomas paid Richard Thomas (and later, his widow) of Pwllypant Farm, Caerphilly £1 10s for service of a stallion. The farm had an annual certificate of exemption from licence duty for two dogs.

Unfortunately, the only evidence available concerning the income of the farm during this period is the sale of 16 sheep (lambs?) for £1 10s each to *J Evans of the Gwalia Stores, Trelewis*.

Extracts from wartime issues of Merthyr Express

Sergeant E. Moss of Welsh Guards

Merthyr Express October 23 1915

Sergeant E. Moss of Welsh Guards has been posted as missing.

Son of Mr and Mrs Moss of Trelewis, he wrote home Oct 12 – *Once again I have the chance to scribble a note to you. I have just heard of Frank Parry* [his name is on Trelewis war memorial]. *He got left in a dug-out between the Germhuns' line of trenches and ours, together with some other chaps. They brought two prisoners back from there, I am told. He, like me, two other sergeants, a captain, and about 23 men, was given out as missing after roll-call that Tuesday morning. We went into a cellar to wait for an officer to come along so that we could find which way our lot had gone, they practically blew the house and a church opposite down on top of us; we had to dig a way out with our entrenching tools. It was awful. We were expecting the place to come in on top of us every minute.*

When we got out and found our boys we were just in time to see them bringing our captain in. He has since died. He was a fine man – Captain O. Williams. We have been in the trenches two or three times since then, but compared with that day it's been a picnic. The artillery still bang like blazes at one another. As far as I know all the boys from Treharris are all right. We have been in dug-outs for nearly a week now. Quite decent places, too, barring when they start shelling you.

Private E. Willett, South Wales Borderers, of Henry Street, Bargoed

Merthyr Express November 6 1915

Pte E. Willett of SWB returned from Dardanelles with left arm blown off almost to shoulders – he told reporter *We made charges for Hill 70, Chocolate Hill, and Hill 50. About 600 yards of trees and bushes had caught fire from shells and bombs, and our regiment advanced through this. We advanced half a mile and captured the first line of trenches, and then the enemy directed machine-guns on us from the hills and most of our officers got killed. We captured Chocolate Hill, however, and it was about halfway up this hill that I was struck, and the bullet blew my arm off. I got back to the dressing station, and was subsequently taken home.*

Bargoed Soldier's Philosophic Letter
THE SPIRIT OF TOMMY ATKINS
Merthyr Express August 11 1917.

According to all testimony, the depression of pessimists at home bears a striking contrast to the buoyant and cheerful spirit of the British soldiers who stand the brunt of battle on the Continent. There might be a tonic for the drooping spirits in the following epistle received by our Bargoed correspondent from Private Oscar Williams, of the Cheshires, who is now in France:

By the time you get this letter, I shall be showing the Germans the result of my training. As I write, I can hear our guns strafing, and how the dickens Johnny sticks it, beats me. No wonder he (Johnny, the German) is windy by the time we get at him. And you can take it from me, Johnny is ready to be taken prisoner any time to get out of it. The one thing that has struck me most out here is the way in which the British Tommy takes things. Nothing deters him. He gets plenty of hardships out here, but bless your heart, the way in which he takes them would surprise you. And you must remember, these chaps represent all classes of people. There's no distinction out here, we all get the same grub, the same bed, the same hardship, and there's a smile on everyone of them that you could not knock off with a sledge-hammer. Well, I would like to say more, but time won't permit. Kindly remember me to Bargoed. I trust before long this horrible 'bis' will be over, and then you will see what kind of boys come home. Wait till the boys come home. In the meantime, cheer oh! we're winning .....

Private Williams will be remembered as a former operator at the Palace [cinema], Bargoed, and afterwards as a worker on the surface of the Bargoed Collieries. He was transferred from the Monmouthshire Regiment on reaching France.

Gelligaer Sanitary Inspector in India
INTERESTING LETTER
Merthyr Express September 21 1918

Gunner H. J. Brown, of the R.G.A. (formerly a sanitary inspector under the Gelligaer Council) writes interesting letters to Mr. Rees Davies, manager of the Council Stores, Gilfach, Bargoed, from Rangoon, Burmah.

My people forward me the "Merthyr Express" every week, which helps me considerably to follow the doings at home. It has given me great pleasure to notice your name in its columns on many occasions in connection with local benevolent movements. Stick at it! Everybody could find something to do if they so desired, couldn't they? ..... I notice that the health department is getting a very important one, with its health visitors and clinics. Well, I don't think they came before they were required. Regarding myself, I may say I am feeling very fit. Our duties out here are not very arduous, and we get everything we require. Of course, the war has not affected the organisation of things out here as it has in Blighty. Everything was done with a rush there, and I used to find that it was a makeshift from beginning to end; but not so here. Every man has his own little bed (not board) and bed-clothes, a locker for himself, and a decent kit – not thrown at him – and plenty of opportunity for washing: and the food is not bad at all. You may be surprised if I tell you that at Christmas we all sat down to a ten-course dinner served up in some style. It was far from being the dinner I had anticipated having in the Army. I am sure it is one of the best I have ever partaken of. This is a fairly interesting country, and warm, of course. We are now at the Fort on the banks of the Rangoon River – a short river trip from the city. Behind us there is nothing but rice fields, and away to the left is a jungle full of monkeys (it makes one feel quite homely!) It is very interesting to watch the Burmese working on the rice; this is a great country for rice .... The implements used are very primitive, indeed; wooden ploughs and bullock carts, just as in the year of one. They cut the rice about 1½ feet down from the top, and it grows to about three or four feet, most of the stalk is left in the ground. That which is cut off is gathered into a great heap, and nearby a clearing is made, about 10 yards square. Then they strew the rice on the path, and drive buffaloes and oxen over it until the grass is all trampled out. Most of the stalk, that part which is left in the ground, is burned at night. It is not a bad sight to see whole fields on fire.

.... I have received several letters from the boys, Dai Harris, Rees A. Davies and Len Morgan...... I should like you to remember me to all the folk, Mr. Gabe, and the rest, and if at any time you have nothing to do, and find time hanging heavily, you know I should be most pleased to receive a line from you, "For Auld Lang Syne".

In the subsequent letter Mr. Brown says:

I have recently spent a few months in hospital with an attack of dysentery. I was admitted on April 17. It was a very severe attack, and I came very near going under. A message was sent to my commanding officer that I might not live; but I recovered although it has been a slow process. When I was discharged from hospital I applied for a month's furlough, and got it. I went for my holiday up to the hills, and stayed in a school in connection with the American Methodist Mission. I had a great time. The school is situated right up in the hills in the jungle. I was 28 miles from the nearest station. I was met at the station by the principal of the school, and the journey was done by motor. Oh, and wasn't it grand! It baffles description! Up and up we went, the road winding in and out between the peaks; there was hardly 50 yards of it straight. Then we would be enveloped in the clouds, being hardly able to see the road – then they would sail by and leave us. When we were near the top we were able to look down on them – floating clouds through the valleys below. It was magnificent! I think the scene was the grandest I have ever viewed. My stay at the school was very enjoyable – good company, plenty of books, and good food. It was a happy retreat from Army life, I can assure you. When I returned I was put in the quartermaster's office on clerical work .... I am glad to know the staff (of the Council) are all well. Please remember me to them.

NB The spelling Gelligaer is used throughout the above, although, in the second decade of the twentieth century, the form Gellygaer was commonly used in reference to the parish, village and local council.

Bargoed Returned Prisoners of War
STIRRING STORY
Merthyr Express December 14 1918

Private W. J. Williams, 17th Welsh, is the first prisoner of war to return to Bargoed since the signing of the armistice. He is well known as a comic singer in the "Metropolis", and amongst his friends is referred to familiarly as "Little Tich". Following is his story: --

I joined up in January, 1915, proceeded to France in the following June, took part in engagements at Gouizecourt, Arras, and other sectors, and was captured at Bourlon on November 24th 1917. I was taken to some village, and they made me carry a machine gun and magazine on my back for 18 kilometres. We got to a place called Lequesnoir, and after six days of proper starvation we reached Munster, Westphalia. We were taken to this camp in horse wagons -- 40 of us in each wagon – and we were only allowed to go out of them twice in three days. We had one meal in three days, and the majority of the men were suffering from dysentery and other diseases. You can imagine the awful state we were in, when I tell you that many of the poor chaps died before we reached our destination – five died in my wagon. When we got to camp several fellows had to be taken to hospital. During our six weeks at Munster we had a 4lb. loaf per day between 12 men, and for dinner we had soup which was simply cabbage water. I shall never forget Christmas, 1917, when we had cabbage water *for dinner, and the German brigadier in charge wished us a Merry Christmas.*

On January 17th, 1,300 of us were collected from various parts of the camp to form a working party for Belgium, and eventually we landed at Lille, where our rations were a quarter of a 3lb. loaf per day and a small bowl of soup. After four or five days we went to a place called Callenelle, and for two days were without anything to eat because the rations had not come up from Lille. They, however, allowed the Belgians to gather some carrots and swedes to make some kind of soup for us.

At a place called Hellam the Belgian people formed a kind of committee and were allowed to give us a bowl of soup a day extra.

At this place we broke up into small parties of about 50, and were supposed to go to work on farms, but instead of that we were forced to carry shells to munition wagons. Anyone who refused to do this work was to be shot. We made a protest and an appeal, but the response from the commanding authority was that the sentry was to shoot anyone who refused to do this galling work. We were always under shell fire. We then moved up to Tournay, and after nine days' work on a quarry we were taken to Lecelles to carry munitions to wagons. This was during the German advance which commenced on March 21st. Towards the end of July all the parties were gathered together on a muniton dump, where the bread ration rose to threequarters of a loaf per day. In this place 20 boxes of biscuits were sent to prisoners of war, so they stopped our bread rations and issued these biscuits, which they said they had captured, at the rate of ten for every two days. From Delmenz we started pulling "Jerry's" transports, 20 men to a wagon, when the Germans had to retreat before the brilliant onward march of the Allies. We were pulling these wagons for a month, sleeping in old barns, on the roadside, or anywhere we could, until we reached Halle, a place outside Brussels, where we heard the news that an armistice had been arranged.

THE TERRIBLE MARCH

On the following day we were told we were to be taken to our own lines by the 26th Division of the German Army. They marched us about two kilometres outside Halle, and told us they were leaving us to go forward on our own until we got in contact with the 26th Division, which they said would meet us and take us to the lines of the Allies. We were a party of 150 starting, and we walked for two days from Brussels to Ath, and then reached our own lines. This was a terrible march. We had no guide, and were expecting all the time to meet the 26th Division, which we never saw.

94

We were sent off without any rations at all, and many of the boys who could not stick it dropped and died on the roadside from sheer want, exhaustion and exposure. We were in such a terribly wretched condition when we got to our lines that our own soldiers did not at first recognise us. But once they did they poured their hearts out to us; some of the boys threw their rations to us and cigarettes, and showed us great kindness. I am convinced it was never intended we should see a German division to lead us to our lines. I attribute my preservation through this memorable tramp to the kindness of a Belgian family who took me in overnight, provided me with a welcome shelter from the cold, a comfortable bed to rest on, and insisted on my taking more than a generous share of the little food they had.

Death is too Good for the Germans whom I saw carrying out acts of cruelty and brutality too hideous to record. I saw German soldiers strike down with the butt of their rifles young girls and children who brought food to our boys. On one occasion I picked up the fag-end of a cigar – for we never had smokes, except the discarded bits of cigarettes and cigars we picked up – and asked a German sentry if he would give me a light. In response he stuck me in the cheek with the spike of his jack knife. That is a good indication of the German character and his disposition towards us British.

There were exciting and violent scenes in Brussels when the news of the armistice came. It was perfect hell. German soldiers threw away their helmets and arms and wore red ribbons as the colours of the republic. Civilians bought rifles and machine guns from some soldiers and were soon in open conflict with other bands of soldiers. Civilians and soldiers cared not what happened, and the scene is beyond my power to describe it.

Bargoed Musician in France
ARMISTICE CELEBRATIONS
Merthyr Express December 21 1918

Mr. Terry Williams, the well known baritone, of Bargoed, manager of the Apollo Glee Singers, and manager of Hodges, Clothiers, establishment, Hanbury-road, writing to our representative from France, where he has been for many a long day, says:

The all-glorious news (meaning evidently the armistice) has given us new leases and we feel too glad to express ourselves. I shall not forget for many a long day the scenes of rejoicing and demonstrations that followed the receipt of the news. I think every device for sound-spreading was put in motion – all sorts of town sirens, hooters, whistles, etc. – broke forth at the same time. It was truly a "perfect day"; the day we have longed and

95

prayed for, and what a privilege we consider it to have seen it dawn. If we could but hear the glorious chorale of praise and thanksgiving that the heartstrings of civilised humanity sent forth! Even the greatest masterpieces of the great masters would bow in respect. Since "Toriad y Dydd" (the breaking of the day) we have been giving vent to our feelings in music, song and dance. Our "superiors" have made it a "red-letter day" for us all. As a member of the concert party, I have been fully occupied, but the immense pleasure I have had in trying to entertain the gallant boys will ever remain fresh in my memory. We gave seven concerts last week, and I am pleased to say our efforts were more than successful. Tommy is ever ready to express his appreciation; and the many thousands who attended our concerts fully revealed their love for good class music. I have been more than interested to read of the recent complimentary concert to my old friend and co-worker, T.R.W.L. (Mr. T. R. W. Lewis, conductor of the Apollo Party). I look back with much pleasure at our cordial unity in the interests of the Apollo, and to him alone is due the honour and credit of our standard of efficiency. Personally, I appreciated very much his constant confidence in my minor efforts at fixing up the many applications for our services, I shall be very happy when I can again meet the old circle.

Mr. Williams enclosed a programme of a concert given by the "Merry and Brights" at the 22nd General Hospital on November 27th, in which he figured prominently, his musical contributions including "Three Green Bonnets" and "Down Here", and in the duet "Flow Gently, Deva", in association with Will Thornton.

ESCAPED SENGHENYDD.

Having survived the horrors of the Senghenydd explosion, Rifleman George Herbert Rees, of the 3rd Battalion Rifle Brigade, has gallantly given his life for his country. Rees was one of the few lucky ones who escaped out of the Senghenydd mine on the morning of the explosion in October, 1913. He is now reported to have died of wounds received in one of the battles of the Aisne, and was buried in France. Rees was 32 years of age. He was the son of the late Thomas and Ann Rees, of Grangetown, Cardiff, and later of Field-street, Trelewis.

Glamorgan Gazette December 4, 1914

At Duty's Calls

Cheer up, dear lass! though we must part
You would not have me stay—
I go to fight 'gainst tyrants' might,
And Honour points the way?

Postcards from World War 1

The card on the right has a postmark date October 16 1916

The card on the left has no postmark. It has a written message:

Sweetheart Mine the world is weary,
when you yet are far from me.
Days seem long my heart is lonely, When your face I cannot see.
A.T.(?)

God Keep You.

An unused string in Memory's Harp,
Was softly touched to-day,
And thoughts of you, came crowding fast,
God keep you dear alway.

97

Greetings

« Ten to one it's over by next Christmas anyway ! »

F. Ifolm

A 2ⁿᵈ sentimental card on the left.

But not all cards were sentimental as shown by the card on the right.

FAREWELL! MY SOLDIER BOY! (3),

Far, far away in homeland, the soldier's sweetheart wept,
While on the field of battle the weary soldier slept;
In dreams he saw the cottage door,
And heard her words of cheer once more.

98

Putting yourself on a postcard was not unusual – perhaps the equivalent of today's Facebook.

On the left is Ollie

On the right is Will Lewis of Cwrt-y-Celyn, Trelewis of Ammunition column, 120th Brigade, RFA, Dec 1st 1915

99

Above: Another personalised postcard, this time displaying two soldiers who were no doubt serving together, but it is not known who they are.

Below: A sentimental card, postmarked 2nd September 1918.

The postcards on these pages are, with one exception, from the family collection of Gelligaer Historical Society member Ella Shorey and are reproduced with her permission.

Wartime visits by emigrants

Annie Owen

The decades preceding the start of the Great War witnessed some emigration from this part of upland Glamorgan to many distant places for a wide variety of different reasons. From late 1914 onwards, the war brought some of them back to Europe and the opportunity to use periods of leave from service to visit friends and family they had left behind in communities across Gelligaer Urban District. What follows are cameo studies of some emigrants whose visits to their former homes are chronicled in the pages of wartime issues of *Merthyr Express*.

James Herber Evans

Born about 1884, James Herber Evans was second of the seven children of Trelewis grocer and local councillor Jonah Evans and his wife, Elizabeth, and, like his older brother, John Sidney Evans, he served in World War I.

Having started his business in Trelewis before the 1881 census was taken, Jonah Evans had a substantial retail concern by the time of the 1891 census when James Herber was a school pupil, presumably attending the local elementary school. Perhaps Jonah Evans encouraged his children to learn the skills required in the family business as, according to the 1901 and 1911 censuses, several of them, including James Herber worked in the business. James Herber was a shop assistant in 1901 and by 1911 he had become a butcher in the business.

Sources studied to date have not shed light on when and why James Herber left Trelewis for Australia, but wartime issues of *Merthyr Express* (June 5 1915, May 13 and 20 1916 and March 3 1917) provide some insight into his enlistment in Australia, service in Gallipoli and France as well as wartime visits to Trelewis.

After enlisting in Australia, Sergeant James Herber Evans, part of the Welsh community in Melbourne, had a hearty send-off when, on April 10 1915, about 250 people gathered in Melbourne's St. David's Hall. They enjoyed a supper with speeches and music, mostly delivered by Welsh emigrants, and witnessed James Herber Evans receive a purse of gold, pipe and engraved gold-mounted tobacco pouch from Melbourne Football Club and a silver matchbox from Williamstown Ladies.

James Herber Evans joined the Australian contingent and served on the Gallipoli Campaign without injury. After that, he was sent to France where he was promoted, from Sergeant to Second Lieutenant, on the field, for conspicuous bravery. Later he was promoted to full Lieutenant.

Well-known in Trelewis, James Herber Evans visited his birthplace at least twice (May 1916 and January 1917) during the war years. Trelewis was a small coalmining community with a population of just under 1,000. By mid January 1915, *Merthyr Express* reported that some 110 young men had left Trelewis to serve their country. Local residents noted that such patriotism was evident not only when, at the end of the working day, the usual haunts of the young men were empty, but also mothers' conversations focused on the whereabouts and welfare of their boys.

It can only be imagined how Sergeant James Herber Evans felt when, accompanied by Australian Private Patrick Colone, his friend since they enlisted in Australia, he visited Trelewis during his furlough in May 1916. Together, Sergeant and Private attended a smoking concert organised by the local Reception Committee at Bontnewydd Hotel. Sergeant Evans was welcomed home with the customary 10 shillings donation for serving soldiers but, like Lance Corporal W. Lewis of Cwrt-y-celyn Farm, home on sick leave from hospital, he returned it with the wish that it be given to local soldiers who were in greater need. As a member of Major Dowdeswell Lodge R.A.O.B. Nelson, he told of the warm welcome accorded him by the Australian Buffs when he first arrived in the Antipodes. Before returning to the Front, Sergeant Evans received other tokens of appreciation including a handsome pipe and tobacco pouch from the ladies of Ebenezer Sewing Class.

Rev. Moses Solfab Young (1883-1959)

The Baptist pastor known as Moses Solfab Young was the popular minister of Fochriw's Noddfa Welsh Baptist Church from 1909 to 1912. Although he was born in Rhondda Fawr, his parents were born and brought up in Pembrokeshire where their respective families had probably lived for generations. Before the 1871 census, his father, like many others in rural west Wales, was drawn by the promise of a better lifestyle in Glamorgan's expanding industrial communities. While his father and older brothers worked in the coal industry, it is not clear whether or not Moses did so. However, he had some experience of farm work as, before 1901, his father had taken the family back to Pembrokeshire where Moses and his younger sister were working on the farm that had formerly been operated by his maternal grandparents and uncle.

It is not clear when Moses Young decided to leave farm work, nor where he trained for the Baptist ministry, but he started his ministry in Fochriw's Noddfa Welsh Baptist Church in 1909 and, at the time of the 1911 census, he was a 28 year old Baptist minister and boarder in two rooms at 17 Aelybryn, Fochriw.

It was not unusual for Welsh men, especially ministers of religion, of that era to adopt an additional name, to ensure certain identification and to maintain a link with their family home. Moses Young probably added Solfab to his name during the first decade of the twentieth century.

In 1912, having married local girl, Gertrude Mary, daughter of Mr and Mrs James Williams of Brynawel, Rev. Young left Fochriw for U.S.A. and his new church, Slatington Baptist, Pennsylvania. The newly-married couple, passengers on SS Mauretania, arrived in New York September 6 1912. War did not prevent Moses Solfab Young and his wife visiting Fochriw: Gertrude left New York on board Finland and arrived in Liverpool June 24 1916, and was followed by Moses who, on board Baltic, arrived in Liverpool August 4 1916. They travelled back together on board SS Adriatic and arrived in New York October 5 1916.

America's entry into World War I brought Rev. Moses Solfab Young back to Europe again. *Merthyr Express* (January 26, June 22, July 13 and October 19 1918) reported on his activities. As Secretary of American Y.M.C.A., he was given six months leave of absence from his church in Pennsylvania. He travelled with the American troops to France, arriving in Paris January 9 1918 before leaving that city on January 16 for a place near the Front. He spent most of his time in the trenches amongst the American troops, but, having been gassed, he was given seventeen days leave in June 1918 during which he visited Fochriw. On returning to his HQ in London he received appointment as religion and social director of all the Y.M.C.A. camps in south west England and south Wales. No doubt, his former congregation in Fochriw was pleased to welcome him back to take services on a Sunday in October 1918.

Following the conclusion of his ministry in Pennsylvania, he returned to Wales in 1920 to serve the Baptist cause by ministering in Cwmcarn (1920-1928) and Bethany, Treherbert (1928-1932) before moving to Grangetown, Cardiff in 1932. His wife, Gertrude Mary, died in Cardiff September 11 1955. When he died January 15 1959, he was survived by his second wife, Chloe Clotthilde Parry, who he had married in 1956.

Samuel Jayne

Born about 1882, Samuel Jayne was son of John Jayne and his wife Gwladys. He grew up in Trelewis and was probably educated in the local elementary school before, like many of his contemporaries, starting work as a coal hewer. As a young man he was well-known in the local community especially for his skills as a footballer. His reasons for emigrating to South Africa are unclear, but may well have been linked with hopes for a better lifestyle as a miner. He was one of several miners from Wales on board Walmer Castle which, April 3 1913, left Southampton for Natal.

Research to date has not shed light on when he joined the colours in South Africa but *Merthyr Express* April 27 1918 reported him missing, only for the following issue (May 4 1918) to inform that he was a prisoner of war in Germany. This was a worrying time for his family in Trelewis, especially as his brother Private Daniel Jayne (Private 6426 of King's Shropshire Light Infantry 5th Battalion) had been killed in action on the Western Front September 1917. It was nearly a month after the Armistice was signed that his parents received a telegram informing them that Private Samuel Jayne of South African Infantry had arrived in Ripon from Germany where he had been held as prisoner of war. According to reports in *Merthyr Express* (October 16 1915, January 8 1916 and May 6 1916) his brother Daniel had visited Trelewis during periods of leave from service on several occasions, but sources studied to date do not show that Samuel had done so. However, to the great relief of his family and friends, he returned to Trelewis in December 1918 as he was in the audience at a smoking concert reported in *Merthyr Express* December 21 1918

OVERWORK AND WORRY DRIVE A HARD BARGAIN.

It doesn't pay to defy nature's laws. We all need peace of mind, rest, outdoor exercise and eight hours sleep to keep well. We must not overeat, nor drink much, unless it be milk or water. These are both good and should be freely used.

Anything bad leads to trouble. Bad habits are no exception. Careless living and overeating are among the worst— they help load the blood with Uric Acid poisons. The kidneys act as safety valves, filtering the blood and passing off the poisons, but they are bound to weaken under any long continued strain, and once they falter, you feel dull, tired and nervous. Your back aches, you lose weight, you have headaches, dizzy spells and urinary disorders.

The first thing to do is to get back to simple, sensible habits. Eat less, sleep more and be careful what you drink. But you must also help the weakened kidneys. You can rely on Doan's Backache Kidney Pills for this help. They are a special medicine for the kidneys and bladder only. That is why so many people recommend Doan's.

All dealers, or 2s. 9d. a box, from Foster-McClellan Co., 8, Wells Street, Oxford Street, London, W.

Stress – a hundred year old problem

Monmouth Guardian and Bargoed and Caerphilly Observer – December 31, 1915

Captain Edwin William Sidney Martin

Royal Army Medical Corps
9th Battalion, Worcester Regiment,
Died of wounds February 16, 1917 aged 41.

Royston Smith

South Wales Echo, Tuesday, February 20, 1917
Death of Brithdir Doctor

"News was received last night that Dr. E.W.S. Martin, Brithdir, who was on active service with the Royal Army Medical Corps, had died in Mesopotamia. Dr. Martin had a large practice in New Tredegar, Brithdir and Cwmsyfiog, and was medical officer for the urban district. He was highly esteemed, and his death is deeply regretted."

The second of four children, E. W. 'Sidney' Martin was born September 18th, 1874, to grocer John Edgar Martin, J.P. and wife Margaret nee Guiney of 41 Church Street, in the small market town of Dromore in the Banbridge District of County Down, Northern Ireland. Sidney received his early education at the National and Intermediate Schools at Dromore and subsequently studied at Queen's College, Belfast. He matriculated in 1892 and enrolled in Physics, Chemistry, Zoology, Biology, Anatomy and Practical Biology; in his last year he studied Sanitary Science and Midwifery. He graduated in 1899 taking the degrees of Bachelor of Medicine, Bachelor of Chemistry, with Bachelor of the Art of Obstetrics.[7]

UK Medical Registers show that the newly qualified young doctor went to Wales. His first post was at Tynewydd, in the Ogmore Valley as assistant to Dr Williams, of Bryn Siriol, where he soon became very popular among the mining communities.

The workmen and officials of the Aber, Wyndham, Tynewydd and Ocean collieries, bestowed many gifts to him at a presentation held in his honour at the Workmen's Hall, Tynewydd on his departure from the area in 1903. According to a report in *Merthyr Express* (September 26th 1903) he was the recipient of a steriliser for instruments and dressings, morocco leather bag to carry same and a case of knives; a valuable microscope with oil immersion lens; a purse of sovereigns; an amputating case, aspirator, tonsil guillotine, stomach pump, laryngoscope, and artery forceps. Dr. R A Williams made a personal present of an obstetric bag and instruments. A presentation in today's value in excess of £7,000, which showed the high

---

[7] Courtesy of Ian McManus, Student Records Office, Queen's University

regard in which he was held.

On leaving Ogmore Valley, Dr. Martin arrived in Rhymney Valley and took up residence at 'Leargaidh' in East View, Brithdir with the surgery at the back of his home.

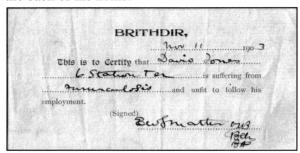

The doctors slip dated 11 Nov 1903 sent to headmaster Samuel Davies to cover the absence of David Jones, 3rd Year Pupil Teacher, for three days due to illness. (Details from the Brithdir Mixed School Log Book 1893-1915)

He built the practice into a large industrial one with the addition of surgeries at Cwmsyfiog and New Tredegar. In October 1905, Dr. Martin, one of the busiest practitioners in the valley at the time, secured the prestigious Diploma of Public Health at Cambridge.

He employed Dr. Walter Mooney (native of Liverpool trained in Ireland) as his assistant and, Sydney William Saxby Organ (of Clifton, Bristol) as dispenser. Mary Ann Jones of Crumlin was housekeeper.

References in newspaper reports and army service papers reveal that Sydney Organ was an interesting character. A regular and prolific scorer for the village football team he was also Dr Martin's assistant in teaching an ambulance class at the Brithdir Council Schools throughout 1909. At a function held in the George Inn to mark a successful class, Mr Samuel Davies, schoolmaster, on behalf of the class presented him with a silver-mounted walking-stick suitably inscribed. Held in high esteem by Dr Martin he looked after all the accounts and bought all the drugs and dressings for the practice. After over 5 years in Brithdir, he returned to Bristol in 1913. He attested to join the army in 1915 and in March 1918 enlisted and was accepted for Special Brigade with the Royal Engineers and posted as Chemist. Demobbed in 1919 he lived the rest of his life in Bishopston, Bristol.

During his 15-years residence at Brithdir, Dr. Martin had proved his public spirit in many ways and had greatly endeared himself to the inhabitants of Brithdir. He represented Brithdir Ward on Glamorgan County Council, was a member of Gelligaer School Governors as well as being Medical Officer of Health to Bedwellty Council and Medical Officer to Bedwellty Board of Guardians for New Tredegar District.

Even for a busy man like Dr. Martin, the call of his country proved irresistible, and he willingly placed his services at its disposal. His medal record card shows he enlisted in 1915 with the rank of Lieutenant. He was first stationed at St. George's Hospital in Malta. In a short time he was promoted to Captain on attachment to the 9th Battalion of the Worcestershire Regiment with whom he went to Gallipoli, and was present at the evacuation of Suvla Bay, before moving on to Egypt and Mesopotamia.

In Mesopotamia, the 9th Worcestershire had seen no fighting of any importance during the summer and autumn of 1916. The disastrous campaign for the relief of Kut had left both the opposing armies exhausted and the heat of the ensuing months had been too severe to permit much movement of troops. So both armies, British and Turkish, lay quiet and waited for the cooler weather of winter. Like Gallipoli, conditions in Mesopotamia defy description. Extremes of temperature, arid desert and regular flooding; flies, mosquitoes and other vermin: all led to appalling levels of sickness and death through disease. Medical arrangements were quite shocking, with wounded men spending up to two weeks on boats before reaching any kind of hospital. On November 29th in hot sun and sand the 9th Worcesters and 7th North Staffs together with a Brigade of Field Artillery and a long train of transport, marched north-westward covering the one hundred miles from Amara to the front in ten days with the last stage completed in rain and mud. The march ended on December 8th, at "Twin Canals" a post on a desolate plain where camp was pitched. After three days rest in the camp, the regiment received orders for their part in the forthcoming operations. At nightfall on December 12th they assembled and marched off moving under cover of darkness with as much silence as possible. Seeking what cover the ground afforded by day, they reached their appointed position on the 14th at "Umm es Sa'ad ford" and the troops dug in. Next morning, December 15th, they were met with a sharp fire of shrapnel and of heavier shells but continued their advance to within five- hundred yards of the enemy's position. The troops dug cover, working for dear life as the Turkish bombs and shrapnel rained upon them. The 9th Worcestershire were constantly deployed to take enemy positions before the enemy had time to organize a counter thrust, and during the next week their energies were concentrated on the work of entrenching the new position and strengthening it for defence. The battalion spent their Christmas in the trenches and by January 21st new trenches, row after row were dug to within 300 yards of the enemy's front line.

Postcard by Victorian Artist Harry Payne depicts the Medical Corps at work while the action rages around them.

Battle of Kut-Al-Amara

On the morning of January 25th the British artillery opened a sudden intense bombardment on the enemy and shelled their front and second line defences. Ten minutes later the attacking troops scrambled over the parapets and surged forward. In splendid order the waves of bayonets swept over the open ground under a fierce fire of shrapnel and machine guns. The advance continued until the leading wave was within fifty yards of the shells bursting along the enemy's front trench. Then the leading line lay down and after a final storm of shells, the British guns ceased firing. At once the platoon rose to their feet and dashed forward with bayonet and within a few minutes all resistance was at an end. The enemy's front line had been won. Losses were heavy and Captain Martin was wounded in the action before, in a separate action that followed, he died in an attempt to save a friend who had been mortally wounded.

Worcestershire Regiment History

"On February 15th the Battalion Medical Officer, Captain E.W.S. Martin was killed on the banks of the River Tigris about 4 miles west of Kut. He was killed going to the aid of a fallen fellow officer, 2nd Lieut W.B. Busby who was mortally wounded."

"No medical officer we ever had was more beloved by all, from the C.O. to

the last joined sweeper of the native establishment, no trouble was ever too much for him, no risk to himself ever affected him." written by a senior officer (Vol 2, page 223)

Captain Edwin William Sidney Martin was buried in plot XX1. L. 11, in Amara War Cemetery in Iraq. In 1933, all the headstones were removed from this cemetery when it was discovered that salts in the soil were causing them to deteriorate. Instead a screen wall was erected with the names of those buried in the cemetery engraved upon it. The War Graves records state he was the son of John E. Martin, J.P., of Ridgeway, Newport, Mon.

Mention in Despatches

Captain Martin had been mentioned in dispatches which entitled him to the "Bronze Oak Leaf" to be worn on the ribbon of the Victory Medal. The Emblem and three medals were issued to his sister, Mrs Kathleen Vaughan of "Dromore House", Tredegar, Monmouthshire. He is remembered with honour on the following memorials:

- Dromore War Memorial, Ireland (birthplace)
- Queen's University, Belfast (where he trained to be a doctor).
- Brithdir Cenotaph (his place of residence)
- New Tredegar War Memorial (Cwmsyfiog and New Tredegar were part of his Brithdir practice)
- Tredegar War Memorial (father and sister's place of residence)

Tributes paid to Dr E. W. S. Martin at a Bedwellty Council meeting of February 27th 1917, as reported in *Rhymney, Bargoed and Caerphilly Observer*, March 2nd 1917

Mr. Joshua Tillott, J.P. chairman said: " *a more loyal servant the council had never had. He was admired by all, and cherished by those who came in contact with him. Very many in New Tredegar and district would always honour his memory.*" Mr Edgar Davies endorsed the Chairman's views and added. "*He took a deep interest in the work of the council and the district in general. He was always particularly keen upon the health of the people. They had lost a most valuable officer.*" Mr R. J. Jones said "*he felt there was no better officer in the whole of the valley or one who took a keener interest in the welfare of the people than Dr. Martin had done.*" Mr. Isaac Jones said "*the neighbourhood in general had lost something more than a doctor. The district had sustained a loss which could not well be replaced. He had many traits in his character which could well be emulated by others. In times of extreme pressure or other circumstances he never rose his voice above its even tenor and was at all times most guarded in his statements."*

Monmouth Guardian April 27th 1917

THE LATE Dr. MARTIN, BRITHDIR.

Mr J. E. Martin, J.P., Tredegar, whose son, Captain E. W. S. Martin, Brithdir, was killed in Mesopotamia in February last, has received the following letter from Lieut-Colonèl W. D. Gibbon, of the Worcestershire Regiment:—" I am writing to express, both in my name and in that of the officers of the battalion, our sympathy with you in the loss of your son, who died of wounds on the 16th of this month. Hearing that Lieutenant Busby had been hit and was lying out in the front, Captain Martin unattended went out to succour him. When at his side, he was shot through his head. He never recovered consciousness, and died in the field ambulance the next day. Captain Martin, or the M.O. as we always affectionately called him, had been with us since June of last year. By officers and men alike he was respected and admired. He never spared himself when his help was required. On two occasions in the past two months I myself know that he worked without stopping for 24 hours. Lieutenant Busby was one of his greatest friends here, and he died trying to save a friend."

TOLL OF THE COAL MINES.
LOSS OF LIFE IN THE SOUTH WALES COAL PITS.

The following information, local to South Wales and Monmouthshire, is extracted from the General Report of Mines and Quarries for the year 1914, presented to the Home Secretary by the Chief Inspector of Mines.

Out of 901,385 persons employed underground, 133,924 were employed in Glamorgan, a larger number than in any other county), and 53,048 in Monmouthshire. The numbers employed above the ground were in Glamorgan 23,014, and Monmouthshire 8,612.

The Scotch and South Wales divisions, employing about 53 per cent. of the number of men employed in the remaining divisions, and producing only 54 per cent. of the output, had more than twice as many explosions from the use of naked lights. In the South Wales division there was one fatal accident (one person killed), with 23 non-fatal accidents (two persons injured).

Of the 1,086 persons killed by accident underground, 335 were in South Wales; in addition, 42 were killed in that division owing to accidents above ground. The death-rate throughout the country was 1.19 per thousand persons employed underground, and 1.68 per thousand in South Wales. The proportions among those employed above ground were 0.61 and 1.21. The number of deaths per million tons of material raised was 4.37 for the country and 6.98 in South Wales.

The number of collieries where coal-cutting machinery was employed was 652, including 58 in South Wales; number of machines, 3093 and 131; tons of mineral so produced, 24,274,517 and 634,821.

It is stated that in the South Wales area, under the General Regulations, 1913, there are seven central rescue stations and 141 mines at which rescue brigades are maintained, the total number of such brigades being 317. These figures are larger than those for any other colliery inspection district. Under the General Regulations of 1914 there will be one additional rescue station, and 60 mines served by central rescue stations.

Monmouth Guardian and Bargoed and Caerphilly Observer – December 31, 1915

A Black Sheep

David Carter

Most families have a black sheep, and this story by David Carter reveals one in the Carter family.

In common with many of their late nineteenth and early twentieth century contemporaries, the Carter family left the coal mining area around Paulton, Somerset, for work in the more modern collieries of south east Wales. They settled in Gilfach, living first in a cottage near present day O.A.P. Hall, before moving to Commercial Street.

Faced with a choice between marrying the young lady he had made pregnant or fleeing the country, John Carter, David's great-uncle, opted for the latter. Boarding the first ship available at Southampton, John Carter worked his passage to Vladivostok as a deck hand, before doing the same to reach the silver mines in Argentina. It was not long before he thought that a better future awaited him in Pennsylvania. He left Argentina and settled down in Pennsylvania for a while before joining up to fight in World War I. That took him to Europe where records show he was killed in action.

That was the story handed down in the Carter family. But just over a decade ago, the local librarian invited David to read an email that had arrived at Bargoed Library. The email, from John Carter's grandson, expressed his desire to make contact with members of the Carter family in the area, and opened up the way to a new version of the story.

While much of the story was probably accurate, it transpires that John Carter was not killed in action. Why then do records show that he was killed in action? His grandson set the record straight when he explained that, having placed his own dog tag on a dead soldier on the battlefield (possibly Passchendaele), John Carter sent the other dog tag to the dead soldier's family.

Meanwhile John Carter trekked through southern France and northern Spain before boarding a ship in Bilbao that took him back to America and his life in Pennsylvania. It is not clear whether or not he was married before his war service. He set up a mining company in Pennsylvania and later took his family to Idaho where his descendants now live.

Did it only happen to the Carters?

William John Morgan 1877-1925
The story of his great grandfather
Neil Phillips

Born in Cardiff on Boxing Day 1877, William John Morgan was son of

William Morgan and his wife, Mary Ann (nee Cresswell). In 1881, at the time of the census, he was living with his parents and 10 month old sister at 55 Diamond Street, Roath, Cardiff. Sadly, soon afterwards his mother was admitted to Bridgend County Asylum where not only did she give birth to another daughter, but she also contracted tuberculosis and died. Subsequently, their father took William John and his sisters to live with his mother, Gwenllian Everall, first in Wingfield Row, Bargoed and later in Quarry Row, near Quarry Arms on Aberbargoed Hill.

The above photograph of William John Morgan was taken about 1905, when he was 28 years old.

It is not clear when he moved to 118 Park Place, Gilfach, his address at the time of his marriage to 20 year old Mary Shaw of 115 Park Place, Gilfach, February 9 1914. He had little time to enjoy family life as on January 11 1915, aged 37, William John Morgan voluntarily enlisted for Army war service at Bargoed Recruiting Station. This photograph shows him in his uniform as Driver, service number 671, in Royal Field Artillery. After basic training in Britain, he landed in France on Christmas Eve 1915, where he used a team of horses to move guns and ammunition around battlefields.

William John Morgan suffered

injury, and, probably late in 1917, he was transferred into Labour Corps where his service number was 407452. His war service spanned 4 years and 11 days before he was discharged January 21 1919. His original discharge papers, now in the hands of the writer, show he was awarded Three Blue Chevrons (one for each year of active service abroad) and that he was discharged *Being surplus to Military requirements (Having suffered impairments since entry into the Service).*

This photograph of William John Morgan, the family man, was taken soon after he returned from war. By late 1919, his third child, daughter Lilian Doreen Morgan, was born and, although his health was poor, he resumed his work as a haulier underground.

Aged 47, he suffered a heart attack, November 2 1925, whilst working underground at Bargoed House Coal Colliery and a report in *Merthyr Express* reads:

Fatal Seizure – Whilst following his employment at the Bargoed House Coal Colliery on Monday, William John Morgan (47), a haulier, of Park Place, Gilfach, had a seizure and died in a cabin at the pit top after being taken up. Morgan, who was married, was a well-known local footballer many years ago, having played half-back for Aberbargoed Rugby Football Club. He saw service during the war and received severe wounds. Dr. L. E. Jones attended, but deceased expired almost immediately after the arrival of the doctor.

His burial, in an unmarked grave in Gwaelod y Brithdir cemetery, cost £1. His widow brought up their three children alone and never remarried. On her death, February 21 1978, over 50 years after that of her husband, she was buried in the same grave as him.

World War 1.…...some reflections.
Menna & Carwyn Hughes.

The returning soldier.

Initially and probably like a lot of people, a number of memories were gleaned about this conflict from older family members perhaps fathers, grandfathers or uncles. My father, 11 at the end of the war was at a very impressionable age. He told me of soldiers who, on returning to their homes, either walked straight through the house into the garden without touching anyone or entered by the garden entrance and promptly stripped off their uniforms. Badges and chevrons were removed and the uniforms thrown onto a bonfire. In addition any souvenirs which had been secreted in the uniform, like enemy knives and pistols, were then revealed. The returnee then bathed probably using Carbolic Soap, dressed, and being free of lice, would embrace family members. In some cases where there might be female persons present, a modesty screen was erected around the bathing soldier.

Military names added to local features.

In Bedlinog, an isolated coal tip high above Garthgynydd Farm, was known as Hill 60. Military cartographers frequently used numbers to identify topographical features and Hill 60 was a spoil tip near Ypres, France. During the excavation of a railway cutting, a spoil heap was generated and such a feature was of paramount importance in the fairly flat Ypres Salient. Artillery spotters used them, as well as commanding officers who needed a bird's eye view over the countryside.

Another tip was known as the Pals' Tip. This one, near the former Bedlinog Colliery, was manually converted to produce a flat area the size of a soccer pitch and a much needed recreation area. During World War 1, groups of young men or Pals, joined up as a group and even helped form regiments.

Anzac Cove and William Richards.

In the ill-fated Gallipoli Campaign of August 1915, three Bedlinog men were wounded, two fatally. William Owen Francis and William Quartley died on the same day, August 10th. William Richards survived. All three were members of the 5th Battalion the Welsh Regiment.

William Richards always claimed that he survived because he was assisted when wounded by yet another Bedlinog man, Joseph Henry Phillips. Joseph Henry, as he was generally known, eventually became pastor of the Bethel Pentecostal Chapel in Mary Street, Bedlinog.

William, my uncle, was transferred from the beachhead to a hospital ship and repatriated to St. Bartholomew's Hospital in London. He became fit again for active service in February 1917 and was posted to Alexandria, Egypt. Here he was transferred to the Royal Engineers, qualified as a railway plate layer and worked on the military railway at Kantara. In January 1919 he shipped out on the Caledonia and left military service on February 22nd 1919.

I am extremely fortunate to be able to reveal details of his military service which I was able to obtain via the computer. Parts are difficult to read because of fire and water damage. Around 60% of World War 1 records were destroyed in the London Blitz of World War 2. I include the first page of my uncle's war record which reveals the damage to documents. Not surprisingly these war service records are known as 'the burnt records'.

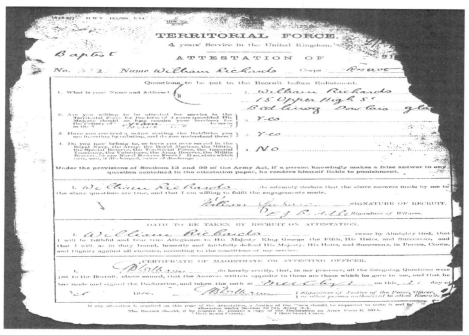

My uncle William was my mother's eldest brother and when he returned from military service she was only five years old. On average, families at that time were much larger than those of today. There were six other siblings born between William and my mother. One of these served in World War 2, as did David Richards, a son of William. Both survived without wounds, but sadly other families were less fortunate, whilst some, even lost more than one son.

Poignant use of a place name.

Philip While named on the Bargoed Cenotaph was a member of my wife's family. He died in January 1916 and is buried in the Merville Communal Cemetery 10 miles north of Bethune, France. During this time the area had a number of military hospitals and in 1940 was the scene of rearguard action leading to Dunkirk.

Philip's parents, David and Johanna While, had another five sons and three daughters. The youngest daughter, born in 1920, was named Merville, possibly after the French village where her oldest brother is buried. Locally her name was pronounced in the English way with the last syllable sounding as ville rather than as the French 'veel'.

Philip left a widow, Alice and a daughter.

From Brisbane to Pontlottyn to Gallipoli.

At the declaration of war in 1914, George Banfield aged 28, left Pontlottyn and returned to Australia, the country of his birth, and enlisted in the Australian Army. His mother, Martha, had emigrated to Australia some years before and married James Banfield in Brisbane. George was their son. After James died, Martha, together with George and her daughter Doris, returned to Pontlottyn and later married John Lewis, a great uncle to my wife. She served the local community as a midwife.

George enlisted in the Australian Army in December 1914 and in May 1915 was posted to Gallipoli. He was to become yet another fatal statistic in that battle zone in the same month.

Unlike the British Army records those of the Australian Army have been retained undamaged, there being no blitz on Australian territory. His mother was informed of his death in September 1915 and he was reburied in the 4th Battalion Parade Ground Cemetery on the Gallipoli Peninsula. His name appears on the Australian National Memorial in Canberra.

The anguish for his mother and family continued for years after his death. Firstly, his private effects were sent to his mother in a brown, paper parcel consisting of photos, letters, coins, wallet, keys, etc. Then, notice was sent that his body had been exhumed from the battle area and reburied. Later, his mother received a memorial plaque and three medals awarded to her late son. All of these continuing to remind her of her loss.

Interestingly, he was survived by a step-brother named Sydney and a step-sister, Adelaide. Thus, the family maintained the Australian connection.

Spanish Flu, a by-product of the war.

Already by the summer of 1918 the effects of influenza were becoming felt in the Somme. Early in the following year it became known as Spanish 'Flu because only Spanish newspapers reported it, whilst other countries censored the information. Returning troops carried the virus all over the world and more people died during the pandemic than were killed in the conflict of World War 1. Some of the army records show that soldiers died of illness and not of wounds, particularly after October 1918.

A sister of my maternal grandfather who lived at Brynrhedyn Farm, Bedlinog, married the local GP, Dr. Frederick Hutchison. In 1898 they emigrated to Canada and helped start the town of Davidson in Saskatchewan, a prairie town out in the far west. Obviously, with his skills, they were a most welcome addition to the community. However, in January 1919 my great aunt, Celia Hutchison, became ill with the 'flu and on February 1st died.

One would have thought that being married to an eminent doctor would have helped to save her, but the virus was no respecter of persons. I have the telegram announcing her death to the family in Bedlinog and the letter from her husband to my grandfather. In it he describes the symptoms of her illness and the feeling of helplessness, when he could do nothing to save her.

Returning soldiers who had been weakened by the rigours of war stood little chance of survival and neither did civilians in good health like my great aunt.

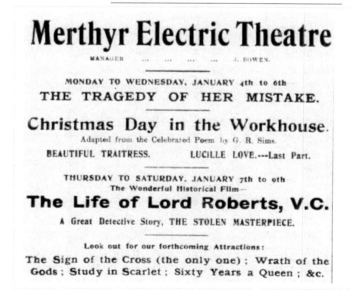

An early Cinema advertisement

(Merthyr) Pioneer January 2, 1915

117

My Family in Uniform

Iris Owens

During the First World War, three members of my family were in uniform: one was a nurse, one a soldier and one in the Rhondda Transport Company.

At the outbreak of the war, Landie Donohue, my mother's elder sister, was a qualified nurse working in Whitechapel Infirmary in the East End of London. Some years previously, she had left her home in Cardiff and moved to London where she trained, also in the Whitechapel Infirmary. It was not long before the heavy fighting in France started and the injured were shipped back to the U.K for treatment. Whitechapel Infirmary was one of the hospitals where the wounded were cared for throughout the war, tended by  the nurses in their stiffly starched white uniforms. All the family, especially her sisters Ethel and Olive, who were schoolgirls, back in Cardiff were very proud of Landie and looked forward to the occasions when she came home with tales of London life. She also told them what the nurses got up to in their free time in the nurses' hostel. Above all they were proud that she was helping wounded soldiers return to health. At some point she was promoted to Nursing Sister, but there are no records to show when this was.

Landie, Ethel and Olive had a brother, Percy Donohue, who had also left home and was living in Tonypandy, working for the Rhondda Transport Company. In 1914, at age 23, he was fired with enthusiasm to join up and fight for his country. Tall and well-built he looked every inch a soldier and wasted no time going to the local recruiting office. He was very disappointed to be rejected for military service on the grounds of having flat feet (which he had not previously realised). The army relied heavily on infantry and any soldier who could not complete long marches would have been a liability to his regiment. With a heavy heart and his flat feet Percy returned to his job at Rhondda Transport and his smart Rhondda Transport uniform.

On a visit to Cardiff on his way to visit his mother and sisters, he was passing Cardiff station when a young woman handed him a white feather, symbol of cowardice, because he was not in military uniform. He arrived at his old home very upset. My mother, his sister Ethel, told me the story first-hand of how he had recounted the event in tears.

Percy Donohue stayed with Rhondda Transport all his working life and rose to rank of inspector.

He is shown in the picture on the extreme left of the middle row.

On 16th November 1914 my dad, Arthur Radley, who had not long turned 15, became indentured as an engineering apprentice to the Mount Stuart Dry Dock Company, for five years. At this time he was too young to enlist in the army, neither was there conscription. In 1916 he passed examinations in Practical Mathematics, Engineering Drawing and Plane and Solid Geometry at The Technical College, Cardiff, as part of his apprenticeship. At some time, however, he was overtaken by events and his apprenticeship was interrupted by military service. His CERTIFICATE

OF EMPLOYMENT DURING THE WAR, Army form z18, shows that he served in the 26th Royal Welsh Fusiliers as a Private soldier in the infantry from May 1918 to September 1919. There were special arrangements made for those, such as my dad, whose apprenticeships had been interrupted. His Indenture certificate shows that despite 16 months spent away at war, it was 'duly fulfilled' in May 1920. Thus he resumed his training and a career in the Merchant Navy as a marine engineer, where in 1925 he obtained his Chief Engineer's Certificate.

In common with many former soldiers he never talked about his war experiences. All I ever knew was that he had been in France. He may well have been in Bapaum and Bethune as the 26th R.W.F were in that area in 1918 and at home we had two letter-openers made from spent rifle cartridges, with those names worked into them. On his z18 form he is described as 'a steady and reliable man', which is how I remember him.

Lawrence Louis Sidney Cook 1890-1964

The story of her grandfather

Marlene Shaw

Born 1890 in Stert, Devizes, Wiltshire, Lawrence Louis Sidney Cook, was ten years old when, with his parents and siblings, he arrived in South Wales. The family lived in Pontypridd for a short time before moving to Treherbert. It was only after World War I that Lawrence, by then a married man, moved with his family to the Rhymney Valley, settling in Tir-y-Berth where he and his wife brought up their eleven children.

I recall as a young child about 5 or 6 years old, how I would clean his war medals. I would happily polish away, shining the four giant coin-like treasures, innocently not understanding then how he obtained them. I remember being told he brought my grandmother beautiful silk scarves from India. In one of

A uniformed Lawrence Louis Sidney Cook with his wife Margaret and their eldest child Sidney Herbert Cook. who was born in 1914.

the drawers of his writing desk he kept a gun, which we children called the 'blunderbuss'. It was in fact a trench flare gun. For writing he would use a wonderful bright orange feather pen, but where exactly he picked this up he never disclosed. I have fond and vivid memories of playing with another article from his war-time deployments, namely a metal spiked German helmet. He never told us how he came by any of these items, possibly because the memories were too painful for him to ever re-tell.

Lawrence regularly played on two harmonicas; one a standard size while the other was a miniature version, just an inch in size! He played them often and incredibly well, a treat we all enjoyed. Looking back I think he probably played them to entertain his fellows in the war time trenches.

A member of both Royal Horse Artillery and Dorset Regiment, he would have been in the forefront and firing line of the battles of the Great War. Only now, as an adult, looking through records and data am I able to recognise and come closer to understanding what he must have gone through, and the sheer scale of the suffering he was unfortunate to be part of. The true horror of what he and the other soldiers suffered, physically and mentally, must have left such brutal scars, especially those unseen to the eyes of the unknowing. Despite his untold torment, he was a wonderfully gentle and kind man.

He was a great family man who loved his children and grandchildren dearly. A very creative and gifted individual, he made wooden toys, leather bags and purses, and, on a more practical level, he would repair local colliers' pit-boots.

Lawrence Louis Sidney Cook on his horse at Curragh Camp, in Ireland, a training camp for soldiers of Royal Horse Artillery.
(photographer Charleton and Sons)

Lawrence Louis Sidney Cook served in India and Egypt.
This photograph may have been taken when he was in Cairo.

121

On the reverse of this postcard Lawrence Louis Sidney Cook wrote *Love from Sid*, Sid being the name Margaret always called him.

He could turn his hand to virtually anything and was certainly a peoples' man in every way. He would help anyone in the community who needed it: the door of his home was always open to all.

In 1926 during the great 'lock-out' strikes he found plenty to fill his enforced spare time. He helped run the Tir-y-Berth soup kitchens alongside his mother and siblings; he became chairman of the local Citizens' Advice Bureau and secretary of Tir-y-Berth Welfare Association, and was an active member of the R.A.O.B. During those years of hardship, he also won a Carroll Levis[8] radio talent contest for singing. He was a well-liked and respected member within the community.

In his later years during World War II, Lawrence worked in the Munitions factory in Caerwent. I cannot but wonder what thoughts went through the mind of this veteran of the Great War as his hands prepared shells and bullets for soldiers in this new conflict, and his sons left, as he had done, to face the enemy.

He was a remarkable and outstanding man, a man who lived and loved life, and I feel honoured and privileged to be his granddaughter.

---

[8] Talent scout, Carroll Levis (1910-1968) was a television and radio personality who came from his native Canada to Britain in the mid 1930s.

Gunner A. P. Cunningham 81568 R.F.A. 1895-1967

Steven Austin Kings

I was born in my maternal grandparents' house of 13, Field Street, Trelewis in 1956, my mother's parents being the only grandparents I knew as my father's parents were long dead before I came along. My family home was in Treharris but being the 1950's both my sister and I were of that generation who were born in the maternal family home.

My grandparents were Austin and Eva Cunningham and as a young lad, together with my sister, we spent a lot of the summer holidays and weekends at 13, Field Street with my grandparents. For myself, there were two attractions apart from spending time with them. Firstly they had a television and the family home didn't. I watched the first Dr. Who (from behind the sofa), Rawhide and Match of the Day all in black and white.

The second attraction was in the front parlour, in a glass cabinet and I was always drawn in to look in the cabinet as soon as I was tall enough to see them. They were 3 medals and a badge lying on display, the medals had colourful ribbons. I knew they were my grandfather's as I sneaked in one day, opened the cabinet and picked a medal up. Inscribed on one of the medals was his name, Gunner A. P. Cunningham 81568 R.F.A., but, no matter how I tried, he would never talk about his war service. He died in 1967 when I was 10 and, although I wondered about his service whenever mention of the war came up, I thought his story was lost.

Fast forward to when I was in my 40's and starting my family history research. I tried to piece together his story and, about 2003, after the second Gulf War, I had access to the National Archives online WW1 service records; well those that survived. Luckily for me, when I put Austin Cunningham's name in the search box, up popped his service record, 12 pages in all. The detail of his postings mirrored eerily the current postings of British troops post Gulf War 2.

Now I had some detail of his personal journey and this is it.

Austin Cunningham was born in Newport, Monmouthshire in 1895, to parents who were in their late 20's when they got married. Thomas Cunningham was an engine driver with the GWR and Mary Harries was a seamstress from Llandeilo. They met when he was lodging in the next house to the Harries family in Garnant. Another son Bernard was born in 1897.

Engine drivers were constantly on the move it seems, as there were a number of addresses on census returns and birth certificates, Newport, Mon, Griffithstown, Mon, and on the 1911 census, Taunton, Somerset which has significance later in the story.

The service record starts on Austin's enlistment day of 15ᵗʰ August 1914, place Bristol as according to the Short Service Attestation he was living at

3, Green Street, Bristol and his occupation was listed as a time served upholsterer. He was assigned to the Royal Field Artillery and given the army number of 81568. Short service was 3 years or until the war was over. By 18th August he was posted to Number 3 Depot R.F.A and by 1st September 1914 he was with 209th Battery, R.F.A.

His medical record on enlisting shows he was vaccinated in infancy, was 5ft 8¼ in height, in good physical condition and was classed as A1.

The next entry in his service record is the Squadron, Troop, Battery and Company Conduct Sheet dated 20th November 1914 where Sgt. Pullen testified that Gunner Cunningham was 2 days and 6½ hrs late back from leave, Major W. Faber confined Gunner Cunningham to barracks for 2 days which appears to be in Camberley

The next part of the service record gets interesting as it's called the Casualty Form-Active Service and lists that he embarked from Avonmouth on 17th June 1915 with the Mediterranean Expeditionary Force. The next entry is that he was in hospital in Alexandria with diarrhoea, this on 10th July and he is discharged 28th July and returned to unit (which seems to have been in Mamoura). His unit then embarked from Alexandria to Gallipoli, he is listed as being with the M.E.F. until 13th February 1916 and from what is known of the Dardanelles Campaign it was not pleasant.

From 14th February 1916 his unit was stationed in Mesopotamia and he was there until 4th March 1919. It seems he had two attacks of dysentery whilst in Mesopotamia and the bases on his record mention Basra and Baghdad which I found very ironic considering the events of 2003 when I found these records.

On 26th April 1918 he was granted a month's leave and embarked for India on 4th May, returning to his unit on 21st July, I guess travelling time was not included so he had a nice long break.

The next entry is dated 2nd February 1919 and he was United Kingdom bound for demob and left on the SS Harding embarking on 5th March 1919 and he was "struck off the strength of the Mesopotamia Expeditionary Force". He was finally demobbed on 31st March 1920 having served 5 years and 230 days and his character is mentioned as Very good.

So, that was Gunner Cunningham's war, I assumed wrongly he served on the hell of the Western Front being in the artillery but he must have had his own experience of hell in Gallipoli and a different war in the Middle East to most.

And what happened after it was over? Despite being a time served upholsterer he never plied that trade again and he became a signalman with the GWR, I suspect his father the engine driver had some influence there.

The last dates on his service record are when his medals are issued and where. 20th November 1920 the 1914-1915 Star was sent to Railway Tce, Abercarn where Signalman Cunningham was lodging. The British War Medal was issued on 25th January 1921 and this time he was in Taunton with his parents. And the final medal, the Victory Medal was issued on 17th September 1921 and he was back in Abercarn.

The medals and R.F.A badge

Austin Cunningham stayed on the railways all his working life and was a signalman at the Trelewis Signalbox. He married his childhood sweetheart, Eva Billings, in Taunton in 1926, the Billings were also GWR people and they lived on the same street in Taunton. By 1929 when my mother was born, the Cunninghams were in Field Street, Trelewis and that was where they lived and died, Austin in 1967 and Eva in 1975.

They had tragedy in their lives, a son died in infancy in 1933 and Bernard, Austin's brother who was also in the R.F.A., died in 1940, supposedly of wounds from the war.

Bernard Cunningham and Austin Cunningham

Although Austin never spoke to me of his war service, he must have needed the company of his fellow soldiers as he was a member of Trelewis British Legion and became a committee member and treasurer. I never saw him on Friday evenings when I stayed over, he was 'down the Legion'. He deserved it and all his fellow soldiers who went through their war.

Stephen Austin Kings
Treharris

127

The Story Behind Ypres, Church Road, Gelligaer

Carol Henderson

Born in Gelligaer village, 8th March, 1882, William James Weeks was son of George and Sarah Weeks. Shortly after his birth, the family moved to Cardiff, where his father worked as a guard on the railway. As his mother died when he was nine years of age, he and his young sister, Florence, then just 1 year old, returned to Gelligaer, to live with William and Margaret Davies, their maternal grandparents. They lived at Old School House, the original site of Lewis Grammar School. It was quite a family household, and, with their mother's five siblings also living there, it must have been crowded. The family was well-known in Gelligaer, with strong links to St. Catwg's Church, as, when he was not working as a collier, William Davies was a church warden and sexton. After their mother's sister, Mary, married William Rhys Morgan, William and Florence lived with her.

While he lived in Gelligaer William Weeks attended both Gelligaer Village School and St. Catwg's Church. Like many other local boys of that time, William left school for work as a collier, probably at one of the small local mines or levels such as Top Hill, Llancaiach, Gelliargwellt (Powell's Works), Pengam or Gilfach.

In December 1899 aged 17 years and 9 months, he enlisted, for 6 years, in the 1st Battalion, The Welsh Regiment, at Cardiff. His enlistment medical describes him as 5'5½" tall, with blue eyes, brown hair and a fresh complexion.

William Weeks sailed with 1st Battalion for South Africa and the Second Boer War in March 1900. He remained in South Africa until July 1904, spending time in Bloemfontein, Johannesburg, Reitfontein West and Pretoria. His Battalion returned to Britain and he was promoted to Corporal and he spent the next few years in the peaceful surroundings of Borden, Hampshire. In December 1909 the Battalion set sail for Alexandria, Egypt, and they spent the next four years in Alexandria and Cairo in Egypt and Khartoum in Sudan. William was promoted to Sergeant on 16th December 1909, and to Colour Sergeant 1st October, 1912. In February 1914 the Battalion transferred to India. After arrival in Bombay they proceeded to Meerut and then on and up to Chakrata, a hill fort above 6000ft in the foothills of the Himalayas. After the heat of the Sudan, the freezing temperatures of Chakrata must have been a bit of a shock.

They were at Chakrata, with the Dehra Dun Brigade in Meerut Division, when war was declared in August 1914. As soon as a territorial unit arrived to take over the garrison, the 1st Battalion, The Welsh returned to England. William was promoted to Company Quarter Master Sergeant on 20th October. They embarked from Karachi on 20th November, 1914, and arrived in Plymouth on 22nd December, 1914, before joining the 84th Brigade, 28th Division at Hursley Park, near Winchester.

After just 3 weeks, they left Southampton for France, and landed at Le Havre, on 18th January, 1915. On 14th February 1915, William was promoted to Company Sergeant Major, Warrant Officer Class II. The 1st Welsh saw their first major action during the Second Battle of Ypres. They were near Zonnebeke, and were receiving hits from a German trench mortar. On 18th April 1915, Lieutenant Henry William Warren Davies, from Milford Haven, was sent out in charge of a party of bombers from B Company, to destroy the Trench Mortar. Aged just 24, he was killed while stooping down to aid a wounded man during the assault, and, as recorded in Regimental History: *Company Sergeant Major W Weeks brought in the body of Lieutenant Warren-Davis and generally set a fine example.* He was awarded Distinguished Conduct Medal and the citation in Supplement to the London Gazette, 30th June, 1915 reads:

8252	Company Serjeant-Major	Weeks, W.	1st Battalion Welsh Regiment	For conspicuous gallantry and devotion to duty near Ypres on 18th April, 1915, in voluntarily going out after an attack and bringing in the body of Lieutenant Davis. Company Serjeant-Major Weeks has previously been noted for his courageous behaviour.

"For conspicuous gallantry and devotion to duty near Ypres on 18th April 1915, in voluntarily going out after an attack and bringing in the body of Lieutenant Davis, Company Sergeant Major Weeks has previously been noted for his courageous behaviour."

Two days later, on 20th April, at Zonnebeke, William Weeks was severely wounded, suffering a gunshot wound to his head. Following initial treatment at the line he was transferred to a hospital in Boulogne and from there to the 3rd Western General Hospital in Cardiff (later known to many as Cardiff Royal Infirmary). His address was shown as The Post Office, Gelligaer, as Ty Catwg was the village post office.

He was promoted to 2nd Lieutenant: 16th March, 1916. Discharged from the ranks and commissioned on 22nd March 1916, William Weeks was transferred to the 3rd Battalion to report for draft. He joined the 2nd battalion on 12th July 1916 and returned to active service in France. He was promoted to the rank of Acting Captain in charge of a company on 9th October 1916 and to Lieutenant on 23rd September 1917. On 3rd February William was sent to be attached to the French in the trenches and on the 17th he led a platoon on a raid.

During the summer of 1917 William married Rosalind Emily Elizabeth Allchorn, at Samford, Essex. It is unclear when he returned to active service in France, but, in March 1918, he was Acting Captain commanding "B" Company 2nd Welsh Regiment, which was holding a sector of the outpost line at Poelcapelle. On 9/10th March, 1918, he was severely wounded (burnt) and suffered respiratory effects from mustard gas shell. Despite his wounds, he remained on duty until his Company was relieved on 11th March, 1918.

The four men being presented with the D.C.M. are shown in the right hand picture, one of them being William Weeks. The centre picture shows one of the recipients receiving his medal. On the left is the presentation party.

Acting Captain William Weeks, D.C.M., retired, on 27th November 1919 on retired pay on account of ill health caused by wounds, and was granted the rank of Captain. He never fully recovered from his wounds and, aged just 46, he died on the night of 23rd/24th August 1928, of pulmonary oedema and cardiac failure caused by mustard gas poisoning. He was buried in St Mary's Churchyard, Langham with full military and Masonic honours. He left a wife and 2 young children aged 7 and 8 years, at their home in Dedham near Colchester, Essex.

The semi-detached houses, Ty Catwg and Ypres, Church Road, Gelligaer were built in 1915, the former for Mary Morgan, William's aunt, and the latter, Ypres, for Florence, William's sister, and her husband, Morgan Price. They named the house Ypres in honour of William's bravery in France. In the late 1940's Mary, by then a widow moved in with Florence and gave Ty Catwg to my father, Glyn Price. My sister, Lynda and I grew up there and, when I married, I moved in with my grandparents. My children grew up living with Florence who died in 1973. My son continued to live there as did my granddaughter. Remaining in the family until the late 1990's, Ypres, Church Road, Gelligaer has been associated with six generations of my family.

Medals of William Weeks:

- Queens South Africa medal and bar.
- Distinguished Conduct Medal,
- 1914/15 Star,
- British War medal,
- Victory medal (Sergeant W Weeks / Captain W J Weeks),
- The Silver War Badge (awarded to those discharged due to their wounds or ill health).

Research: service record, medal cards and 1st Battalion, The Welsh Regiment War Diary.
Acknowledgment: Special thanks to Celia Green, Customer Services Manager, Regimental Museum of The Royal Welsh (also representing 24th Regiment, South Wales Borderers, The Welch Regiment, The Monmouthshire Regiment and The Royal Regiment of Wales) The Barracks, Brecon, for all her assistance.

Albert Joseph Gerrish

Albert Henry Gerrish married his wife Alice in their native Somerset in 1886, and their son, Albert Joseph Gerrish (who became known as Bert to his family and friends), was born in Bristol in 1889. The family was living in Somerset at the time of the 1891 census, Albert Henry Gerrish being employed as a general labourer. While it is not clear when, during the

following decade, the family moved to Rhymney, the move was probably motivated by the promise of work for himself and his son.

Heading a household in Hill Street, Rhymney, in 1901, Albert Henry Gerrish worked as haulier underground in coal mine, while his 13 year old son was a blacksmith's assistant. A decade later, the family was still resident in Hill Street when father and son were both in the employ of a colliery company, father as haulier above-ground and son as electrician.

On January 1st 1914 Bert joined the crew of SS Wandby at Barry. His Continuous Certificate of Discharge sheds light on Bert's career on SS Wandby, 106996, a steam propelled cargo ship built by Ropner & Sons

A young Bert Gerrish with colleagues, probably at Abertysswg Colliery.

of Stockton-on-Tees in 1899. He had seventeen engagements, the first five as 4th Engineer and the others as 3rd Engineer, before his final discharge July 9 1920. As a seaman he was not expected to join the armed forces but

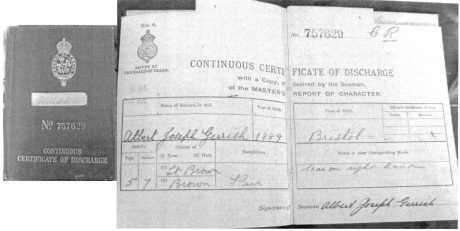

his ship would have been a target of war.

These engagements took him across the seas to a wide range of destinations including Montreal, Baltimore, Alexandria and River Plate. Not surprisingly, many of the wartime voyages were described as *Foreign* or *O.H.M.S.* (On His Majesty's Service). His record of character was admirable: with *VERY GOOD* for ability and for general conduct stamped on each of the seventeen engagements.

Albert Gerish's Seaman's Identification Card
Dated December 28 1918.

Surviving *ACCOUNT OF WAGES* shed light on Bert's earnings and spending during his time at sea and that shown on the right covers his eleventh, twelfth and thirteenth engagements from September 23 1917 to April 4 1918. This seems to show that in a period of 6 months he was employed for only 3 months and 11 days. He earned £20 a month while working so his pay was £67.33. He had evidently taken advances when going ashore at

133

Alexandria, Malta and London. He had also purchased £1.75 worth of tobacco – presumably from the ship's stores. He was also deducted £9 for "Allotments" which refer to allotments of pay. Sailors could allocate portions of their pay to be paid directly to their wives and families while they were away at sea.

While at sea, Bert kept in touch with home as shown by the following postcards:

Making a photograph into a postcard was not unusual in the early 20th Century. This postcard was sent to his parents and sister

Another postcard, with photograph of some of the crew of SS Wandby.

Dai Jenkins, of 2 Garden City, Rhymney, sent this postcard, showing Rhymney's Lower High Street (next page), to Bert to be collected when the SS Wandby called at Naples.

134

Having set out on his final voyage on SS Wandby on April 1 1920, Bert went to the U.S.A. and the Baltic before he was discharged July 9 1920 at West Hartlepool. Soon after, he married Maude I. Davies. It is likely that he met Maude, who was in service at Rhymney's Royal Hotel, before he joined the Merchant Navy. This card and message with photograph inside was probably just one of a number that Maude received during his absence from Rhymney.

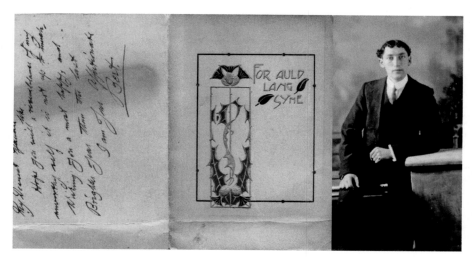

Photographs of some items returned to Bert's family when they applied for his effects.

The first photograph shows some items which puzzle the family. The wooden item at the top of the photograph has CHELLA-PHONE PAT 112368 inscribed on the side opposite the numbers shown, and the narrow end (left) is open. The cloth badges produced by tobacco companies in the second photograph were probably collected by Bert.

Anecdotal evidence in the family suggests that Bert had been tempted by offers of employment, including one on a plantation in U.S.A., before his discharge from SS Wandby, and he may have thought about these offers when faced with the dismal employment prospects in post-war Rhymney. It is not clear if Bert returned to work in the colliery nor when he decided to leave Rhymney for the then thriving town of Bargoed. However, most of Bert's post-war working life was spent as an electrician in the employ of Gelligaer Urban District Council and he was living in Bargoed before his younger son, Graham, was born in 1931.

Less than a year after he had left SS Wandby, the ship, on a voyage from Algiers to Portland, Maine and captained by David Simpson (who was Master during all Bert's engagements from September 26 1916 onwards), ran aground under a full head of steam in a dense fog at Kennebunkport, Maine, on March 9 1921. Since then there have been two further ships called Wandby: one was torpedoed and sunk by a German submarine off Rockall in 1940 and the other was later sold to Greece and renamed. Today what remains of the Wandby on which Albert Joseph Gerrish served attracts shipwreck divers.

Albert Joseph Gerrish died June 29 1955 and now his daughter-in-law, Margaret, cherishes memories of his life and work.

World War I and Education in Gelligaer : Cameo Studies

Annie Owen

On the eve of World War One, both Glamorgan L.E.A. and Gelligaer School Managers, acutely aware of the importance of education, placed great emphasis on creating a sound education framework for the rapidly changing social and economic community. The outbreak of war did not deflect them from that purpose. New elementary school premises, such as those opened in Ystrad Mynach and Brithdir in September 1915, helped cope with the expanding school population as modern collieries at Bargoed, Penallta and Britannia came into operation. At the same time, School Managers discussed curriculum reform in Bargoed Higher Elementary and Pengam and Hengoed secondary schools, while headteachers of elementary schools across Gelligaer Urban District aspired to maintain pre-war standards. However, it was inevitable that, as the war continued, education was affected.

Note on sources

This series of cameo studies, based on sources such as extant school log books and reports in the local press as well as some military records, aims to offer some examples of ways in which the war impinged on local schools, teachers and pupils. There is no attempt to cover every school within the former Gelligaer Urban District.

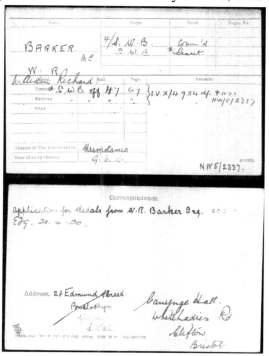

Teachers and war service

As it is not possible to pay individual tribute to all Gelligaer's teachers who responded to the country's needs, the medal card of William Richard Barker serves to represent the valuable contribution made by local teachers. Generally known as Billy Barker, he was born in Warwickshire about 1893, son of timber merchant Frederick Barker.

By the time the 1911 census was taken, 17 year old Billy was a student teacher boarding in 28 Edmund Street, Pontlottyn. He taught in Brithdir and Pontlottyn schools before leaving for war service and some readers may remember him as headmaster of Deri Mixed Primary School in the 1940s.

Inevitably, boys' departments, with almost exclusively male staffs, were more adversely affected than mixed, girls' and infants' departments. Thomas Cornelius Jones' entries in the log book of Gilfach Boys' Department were typical of those in charge of boys' schools-

- *March 1 1915 the continual change in staff is against the interests of the school*
- *December 19 1915* After examining the various classes for three weeks he concluded *the results are not quite up to the standard of last year largely due to the influence and demands of war upon the Staff consisting of Males. The Staff which is an excellent one judged from any standpoint have enrolled under Lord Derby's Scheme with the exception of Mr William Jones and Mr. L. Isaac.* Other entries show that the former was a conscientious objector while the latter suffered ill-health.
- *October 13 1916, I find the discipline in the upper classes suffers under the management of Female Teachers and have to personally remain all day in one of the classrooms in order that work may be carried on satisfactorily*

Re-employment of retired teachers

John Davies and Thomas Myddfai Jones, both former headmasters, came out of retirement to meet the wartime emergency.

After thirty one years as headmaster of Trelewis Mixed School (formerly Bontnewydd Board School), John Davies retired March 31 1913 only to take a post as certificated assistant in Nelson Council School December 1 1914. However, during the following fortnight, headmaster, Evan Thomas Owen, joined the Royal Army Medical Corps, and John Davies was appointed temporary headmaster, a caretaking post that he held until April 30 1919.

In 1913 headmaster Thomas Myddfai Jones wrote in Bargoed Boys' Department log book *Before dismissing the school this afternoon I wished the boys "goodbye" and asked them to be good lads and so grow up to be good and useful men. This is my last entry in this the third log book that I have been spared to use during my fifty years' service.* His place as head was taken by David Davies who, just a few pages further into the log book, wrote (on May 31 1916) *Mr Bryn Davies, County Inspector of schools, called this afternoon and made final arrangements pending my departure for War Service on June 5. Mr T. M. Jones, the former Head teacher of the school, is to take over the charge of the school on Monday June 5th. Also my wife Lily Kirkhouse Davies is to take up duties here as certificated Teacher on that date.* As other qualified and experienced male teachers left for war service, it was not easy for Thomas Myddfai Jones and his staff to maintain educational standards for Bargoed lads up to age 13. Not only does this extract refer to the return of retired Thomas Myddfai Jones but it also mentions employment of married women teachers, in this case the wife of David Davies. Such employment of married women teachers only lasted for the duration of the war and, soon after he returned on January 13 1919, David Davies wrote in the log book: *My wife Mrs L. K. Davies terminated her engagement at the school today* (January 31 1919) *according to the terms on which she was engaged.* In his seventies at the time of his wartime service, one wonders how much Thomas Myddfai Jones' advanced age made his task more difficult and if it contributed to the playground accident or the ten week recovery period mentioned in his log book entry of June 11 1917 referring to his *return to duty after a 10 week absence due to an accident he suffered in the playground on Monday April 2.*

Gilfach Boys' Department

Thomas Cornelius Jones, head of Gilfach Mixed Department since its opening in May 1898, had ensured a commendable standard of education in spite of the problems of severe overcrowding in the school as the local population expanded following the opening of Bargoed Colliery. With new accommodation available in April 1913, the Mixed Department was split into Girls' and Boys' Departments and Thomas Cornelius Jones became head of the Boys' Department. During the war years, while he strove to maintain the high standards that His Majesty's Inspectors had praised in their 1913 report, it became increasingly difficult as qualified and experienced male staff left for war service, and his entries in the school log book show problems with inexperienced and sometimes unqualified teachers, many of whom were female, who replaced the young male teachers he had trained.

Certificated teacher, Arthur Fred Greenaway, had joined the staff from Quakers Yard Truant School just a few months before he volunteered for the Front when the war was only weeks old. In those early weeks of war, his colleagues and the local community expected to welcome him home after a quick and victorious conclusion to the war. However, as 1914 gave way to 1915, it became clear that the quick victory was not to be, and Thomas

Cornelius Jones' entries in the log book reflect the war's effect on the school.

Thomas Cornelius Jones was aware of slipping standards in 1915, and, as the war continued, the real impact of the loss of male staff became increasingly evident as experienced and capable male teachers left. John H. Garnett (described in the log book as an *able and conscientious* teacher who had started at the school as an uncertificated teacher on December 6 1909 before training in Reading College and returning to Gilfach), John Lodwig Evans (an experienced and capable certificated teacher) and Alfred L. Smart (a pupil teacher who had previously been rejected for war service due to defective eyesight) left for war service during February 1916. On May 16 1916 Thomas Cornelius Jones wrote *Today is the last day for Mr Thomas Glyn Jones and Mr William Sydney Griffiths uncertificated teacher as they have been called up for tomorrow the 17th inst ....* and he continued *The changes in staff this year have been very great and of the 4 Uncertificated teachers males whom I have of late trained everyone will have left by tomorrow*.

As the male staff left, they were replaced by females (if replaced at all) and these ladies were often inexperienced as indicated when, on June 5 1916, Thomas Cornelius Jones wrote *Miss Elizabeth Ann (Bessie) Price Certificated Teacher commenced duties today. She is an old pupil of the school, but has had no experience in teaching.* His misgivings proved unfounded as when little over 15 months later, she was transferred to Bargoed Higher Elementary school staff, he wrote *when she came here she was without experience and having become useful she has been transferred*.

As a conscientious objector, long serving teacher, William Jones, was given notice by the L.E.A. and his engagement ceased at the end of September 1916. On September 29 1916 Thomas Cornelius Jones recorded that he *finishes duties today. After this date I shall have two male teachers on the staff both of whom have been rejected as unfit for Class A*. He makes the impact of the war on his school clear when he wrote *since the advent of war, the changes have been very great indeed as the school was staffed entirely by males*.

The weaknesses of some of the female teachers together with understaffing as teachers who left were not replaced contributed towards what, throughout 1917 and 1918, Thomas Cornelius Jones repeatedly described in the log book as '*strain*'. On January 16 1917 he wrote *The vacancy created by the removal of Miss Griffith Certificated Teacher in September last has not been filled, the work is carried on under great difficulties and* **strain** *on the remaining teachers.* The arrival of Miss Susannah Mary

Bowen, certificated teacher, on February 1 1917 did little to help, as she had been trained for infant work and was *new to everything carried on in a Boys' School.* Thomas Cornelius Jones wrote *The latter schools* (i.e. Boys' Schools) *have been hit badly as Male Teachers left are as a rule staffed by inexperienced Females from College The **strain** is great on this account.*

However, as entries in the school log book continued to reflect the headmaster's concern about discipline and academic standards, the word strain appeared again. On May 11 1917 he noted that *the discipline is not what it was with a Male staff and much extra labour and anxiety are thrown upon me as Head Teacher,* and after examining the work of the various classes he wrote on December 9 1917 *I found the work not so thorough as in past years and altho' the teachers work hard the **strain** of controlling boys in a district like this saps much of their strength. The work thrown on my shoulders I find very heavy.*

In spite of his general comments about female teachers, Thomas Cornelius Jones sometimes remarked on the strengths of an individual. On February 18 1918 he responded to the news that Miss Louisa Elizabeth Morgan, a certificated teacher, was going to Cardiff after Easter, by noting *a great loss to this school as she is the most efficient teacher on the staff and has had considerable experience both at these schools as Uncertificated teacher and at Cardiff before going to College for a course of training. The changes of the last year have put a great **strain** on me as head teacher.* In October 31 1918 he noted that Miss Gwladys Tydfil Davies was leaving for a post under L.C.C. describing her as *most regular, painstaking and efficient teacher* and remarking that *her loss will be felt as I am so short of teachers fitted for older boys.*

On July 16 1918 when supply teacher, David John Davies, was transferred to Ystrad Mynach Boys' school, Thomas Cornelius Jones wrote *I am now with only one male on the staff as he is a Certificated Teacher discharged from the Army. As there are 416 boys on roll the **strain** is and has been unduly severe on me as Head Teacher.* He had mentioned it numerous times and it is clear the strain was taking its toll on Thomas Cornelius Jones. Then about 53 years old, he was medically advised *on account of illness* to prolong his summer stay in New Quay and so he returned to school a week after the term had started in September 1918.

The Armistice came November 1918 and by January 1919 the pages of the school log book detail the return of male staff who had left a few years earlier. The first to return was Alfred L. Smart, an uncertificated teacher and former pupil of the school, who recommenced his duties in the school on January 13 1919. He was followed by T. Glyn Jones, uncertificated teacher, on January 20 1919 and W. S. Griffiths, uncertificated teacher, on January 29 1919. On March 4 1919, J. Lodwig Evans, certificated teacher, was the first teacher of experience to return to the school.

When James Tyler, certificated teacher, returned to Gilfach in March 1919, he was welcomed back not only to the school but also by his wife Lena and their infant daughter, Margaret Valerie, in Maesygraig Street. Born in 1916, little Margaret Valerie was one of countless children with virtually no memory of their father before he went to war, but unlike so many, she was able to get to know him when he returned from war service. Having joined the staff on February 10 1908 as an inexperienced teacher who gave good lessons but needed help with discipline, James Tyler had matured into a good teacher and colleague and when he left to join H.M. Forces on March 9 1917 Thomas Cornelius Jones wrote *During the whole period* (ie 9 years) *he had been loyal, hardworking and probably the most efficient male teacher I have ever had on my staff. He leaves with our best wishes for his early return and safe return.* He served as clerk in the Army Service Corps, the huge and effective organisation that supplied the forces on many fronts, ensuring supplies of food, equipment and ammunition were conveyed by horsed and motor vehicles, railways and waterways. This vast sprawling organisation so vital to success, was a massive logistical undertaking which, at its peak numbered 10,547 officers and 315,334 men, as well as tens of thousands of native labourers, carriers and storesmen across the world, and one of the reasons why the war was eventually won.

The return of male staff was complemented by loss of female teachers such as Miss E. M. Williams, uncertificated teacher, who, on January 17 1919, was transferred to the Infant department. To outward appearances the staffing position regained its pre-war status as the school moved into the 1920s, but their experiences had changed the men who picked up jobs they had left before their war service.

Brithdir Girls' Department

While boys-only establishments were vulnerable to staff difficulties during the war years, girls-only schools were not immune to staff problems.

When, in September 1915, Brithdir Girls' Department opened in the premises formerly occupied by the Mixed Department, it had an all-female staff (headteacher and three assistant teachers). During 1915-1916, headteacher Martha C. Price recorded numerous occasions when one or more of her female teachers was temporarily redirected to cover staffing shortfalls in the neighbouring Boys' Department, which had opened in new-built premises in September 1915. One female teacher so deployed was Elizabeth Isaacs who joined her staff October 1 1915 but was transferred for a few days temporary cover in the Boys' Department on January 27 1916 and again on May 22 1916.

When Martha C. Price resigned her headship at the end of 1916 she was succeeded by Mary R. John who also faced staffing problems, especially as some female teachers served short temporary stints of duty. During 1917 she noted in the log book that female teachers were absent when relatives (usually brothers) had home leave from war service. Miss Muriel Davies was absent February 23 1917 as her brother arrived suddenly from the French Front owing to the illness of their mother (wife of the master of the Boys' Department). Sadly the mother died less than a month later and Muriel (and her sister Olwen, a student teacher in the school) was absent for a week. Miss M. Davies, certificated teacher, was absent September 17 1917 as her soldier brother was home on short leave from the Front and just days later (September 21) Miss Margaret Davies went home having received news of death in action in France of one of her soldier brothers. Miss Maria Lewis was absent when the school reopened on October 30 1917 after half term break as her soldier brother was home on short leave, and she left school a little early (at 3.15pm) on June 14 1918 to spend a weekend with her soldier brother home on short leave. The staffing situation was particularly difficult when the school reopened in January 1918 as two teachers had left before the Christmas holiday but were not replaced until several weeks of the new term had passed.

Bargoed Higher Elementary School

In February 1915, J. Sylvan Evans, B.A., first headmaster of Bargoed Higher Elementary School, noted in the school log book that W. H. Evans, Commercial subjects master, was taking up a commission as Assistant Paymaster in the Royal Navy. This extract from *The story of Bargod Grammar Technical School 1910-1960,* a Golden Jubilee celebration of the history and achievements of Bargoed Higher Elementary School and its successors, was written by one of his pupils, Vincent Evans, then Chief Accountant, South Wales Electricity Board:

W. H. Evans
taken from staff
photograph of 1910.

My years at the school covered the early part of the First World War and I clearly recall the visit one day of Mr. W. H. Evans (a former master of the school, and later to become one of H. M. Inspectors of Schools) while home on leave. He was resplendent in his uniform of an officer in the Royal Navy and we pupils were most impressed. I would hazard the guess that the event did not pass entirely unnoticed by the mistresses then on the staff. Other officers who paid visits to the school, and were duly admired in their uniforms, were the two sons of the Head who were doing their bit in the Army.

Two other extracts from messages from former pupils in that same volume shed further light on the school and the war. The first, written by J. Stanley Jones, B.A., Principal, The Mining and Technical Institute, New Tredegar, is about a pupil:

... my friend, Mr Harry Hubert Jenkins, M.M., O.B.E., of Heolddu Farm, Bargoed. He was one of the first group of students to enter the school on its opening in 1910. In the First World War he was awarded the Military Medal for gallantry in France, and in the Second World War, a quarter of a century later, he was awarded the Order of the British Empire for gallantry in the Pacific.

The second, by Idris Jones of Brithdir, Chairman of the Past Students' Association, is about the school caretaker and the school war memorial and, at this point it is worth noting that the building has been demolished and the whereabouts of this war memorial and other tablets is uncertain:

A very well-known character was the school caretaker, Mr. Thomas, who was very proud of the service he performed for the school when he carved and erected the war memorial which is now to be seen in the entrance hall. Arrangements were made for him to have assistants to carry the structure from the boiler-house, where he worked the wood, to the main hall in which the tablet was eventually to be placed; and since I was a tall boy, I had my part in the periodic removal of the unfinished article during the time when adjustments were being made. Mr. Thomas probably regarded this labour as a convenient method of using the boys' surplus energy. I believe the memorial was unveiled in a ceremony in the school concert on the evening of St. David's Day.

Higher education on hold during the war

William Walter Williams of Springfield Villa, Brithdir, was a student teacher at Carmarthen College when he joined 5th Welsh Regiment in 1915. Daniel and Howell, sons of Mr and Mrs George Jones of 8 Station Terrace, Fochriw, also found their academic careers disrupted by the war. Having received their secondary education at Lewis School Pengam, Daniel proceeded to college in Exeter, where he joined the 4th Devons at the outbreak of war, while Howell studied at U.C.W. Aberystwyth. Howell joined R.W.F. in January 1915 and was wounded in action on three occasions. After several months in a Camberwell hospital, he recovered sufficiently to visit his family in Fochriw in October 1916. A year later, both Howell and his older brother, Daniel, were in hospital. Howell, by then Lieutenant in York and Lancaster Regiment, had been wounded in the last big push and was in hospital in Winchester, while Daniel, ill with malaria, was in hospital in Secunderabad, India, where he had been serving for over three years. At that time, a younger brother, Thomas John, a student in Aberystwyth, was in Officers' Training Corps. Howell made satisfactory progress and was able to take a short leave in Fochriw a few weeks later. Having returned to active service in France, Howell was wounded for the third time in May 1918, and, after some time in hospital, was able to return to Fochriw by September 1918.

Thomas Davies Evans, having moved to Bargoed on his father's appointment as first headmaster of Bargoed Higher Elementary School in

1910, completed his secondary education at Lewis School Pengam. There he excelled: in 1912, not only was he Head Boy but also his success in the annual examinations earned him the school's Caldwell Medal and a £30 Glamorgan County Scholarship before he commenced his university course. His brilliant academic career was interrupted when, in the third year of his studies at U.C.W. Aberystwyth, he joined the colours. Early in December 1915, he left for service in France where, he was promoted to Captain on the field. As noted above, pupil Vincent Evans remembered that both he and his younger brother, Iwan Jenkyn Evans, wore their army uniforms when they visited their father's school. After being discharged

145

from his regiment, Thomas Davies Evans returned to university and graduated in the summer of 1919.

Armistice and Peace

Thomas Myddfai Jones simply wrote *Peace. Armistice Terms signed* in Bargoed Boys' Department log book on November 11 1918. Two days later, his namesake, Thomas Cornelius Jones, in Gilfach Boys' Department, wrote *School breaks up today for the rest of the week to commemorate the signing of the Armistice – The 12th was a day in School never to be forgotten.*

David Davies returned to duty in Bargoed Boys' Department on January 13 1919 to take the school into the post-war era. His log book entry on July 22 1919 was lengthy: *Yesterday was a holiday given by the Education Committee for the continuance of the Peace Celebrations of July 19. On Saturday July 19 the children assembled at the school at 12.30 pm in readiness to march through the town. The march was very effective – most of the boys carried flags …. All the teachers were present and marched with the children. After a short service at Hanbury, the children returned to school and were given tea. The arrangements for the tea were very effective. The tea commenced at 3.15. All boys sat to have tea together – over 600 in number. By 3.45 all had finished. Mr Haydn had charge of boiling the water and brewing tea. Mrs Davies has charge of the women helpers at the school. Wet weather after 12 pm.*

Note : Lewis School Pengam

Two written histories of Lewis School Pengam include information about the school and World War One:

- Arthur Wright's *The History of Lewis School, Pengam*, published in 1929, can be read on http://www.lewisschoolpengam.org.uk/
- Ewart Smith's *Lewis' School, Pengam*, a History, published in 2013.

Research into the story of the school and World War One is ongoing as witnessed by:

- *Testament of Youth* by Dic Felstead (in this volume)
- Research, by former Ludovican, Paul Williams, uncovering details of the schools' Old Boys who were casualties of World War One. Anyone with relevant information may contact him on williams.p14@sky.com .
- The school's ambitious Heritage Lottery Funded World War One Project.

The Impact of the Great War on the railways of Gelligaer Parish and adjoining areas.

Terry McCarthy

At 11.00 pm, Tuesday 4 August 1914, the day following August Bank Holiday, the British Government, having received no response to its ultimatum from the Imperial Government of Germany, declared that a state of war existed between the two countries. So began the Great War an 'emergency' lasting for over four years bringing in train significant changes to the economic, social and political landscape from that prevailing before the war.

Gelligaer Parish and its immediate surroundings were not immune from these processes, but to date little has been written about the effects of the 'war to end all wars' on the railway system in this, or any other area in south Wales. A partial explanation might be, that being of strategic significance, reporting of railway operations was strictly censored in the press and even railway companies' Boards of Directors' minutes and reports were so bland they give few hints as to what was happening. Such restrictions did not apply to the railways' emerging competitors, nor their political detractors, thus the few reports which emerge tend to be negative.

This article hopes to shed some light on the role of the railways in the study area during the war years, their achievements, the constraints under which they operated and what the short and medium term outcomes were for this strategically significant, but often (deliberately) undervalued transport system. The sources are many, with information gleaned from Board of Directors' Minutes of the Rhymney and Brecon & Merthyr Railways; reports to the Great Western Railway directors following the war; reports of company annual meetings in both The National Archives and Welsh Railways Research Circle's copies of the late Colin Chapman's transcriptions; newspapers, notably the *Merthyr Express* and *Caerphilly Journal*, journals such as the Railway Magazine and Welsh Railways Archive, plus a wide range of published works.

The study area

The study area, shown in map overleaf, is dominated by Gelligaer Parish, but includes some strategically important locations and railways on the fringes which had significant wartime links with those operating in the parish area. In 1914 this railway system comprised tracks of five main railway companies, plus two joint operations [1]. Even before the war there was a large amount of interchange traffic between the railway companies, which expanded during the war years, mostly involving goods traffic.

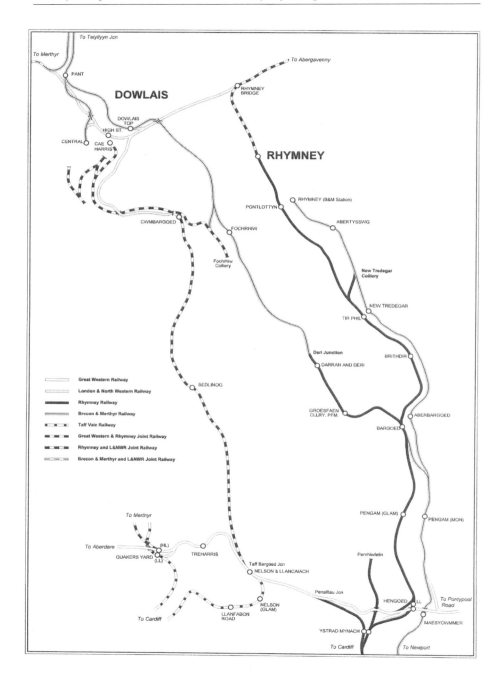

The Pre War Railway network

Railways within the study area were privately owned, legally incorporated companies comprising two main categories: local companies including the Taff Vale Railway (1836) [2], Rhymney Railway (1855), Brecon & Merthyr Tydfil Junction Railway (1858) [3] and two national companies, the Great Western (1835) and London & North Western Railways (1846) [4]. Jointly operated lines included those constructed by the RR & LNWR from Rhymney (1871) and that from Llancaiach to Dowlais built jointly by the GWR & RR (1876)[5]. As a result of agreement reached over the years, most companies also had legal rights to operate over lines of neighbouring companies [6] (table 1):

Powers given to	Over	Route
L&NWR	RR	Rhymney – Cardiff
L&NWR	GWR	Pontllanfraith – Hengoed (then to Ystrad Mynach RR)
GWR	L&NWR	Pontllanfraith – Nine Mile Point
GWR	B&MR	Maesycwmmer Jct. (Fleur-de-Lis) – Rhymney Works
RR	GWR	Penalltau Junction – Hirwaun Pond.
B&MR	RR	Bargoed South Junction – Deri Junction.
RR	B&MR	Deri Junction – Fochriw
Barry Railway [7]	B&MR	Barry Junction (nr. Llanbradach) – Rhymney.

Table 1 – Lines over which running powers were exercised.

Prior to the outbreak of war in 1914, Britain's railways were profitable, providing good returns for shareholders and investing in new capital to enhance the efficiency of their operations. Those in the study area were no exceptions, being amongst the most profitable in the U.K. Traffic in the area was dominated by one commodity – coal. In 1913 south Wales collieries produced 57 million tons of coal, of which 37 million tons was exported, mostly for steam raising in ships and railways. The principal flows were from collieries in the Valleys to the Bristol Channel ports, notably Cardiff, Penarth and Barry, operated by a range of local railway companies, the RR, B&MR and TVR being prime examples. There was a significant west to east flow, mainly worked by the GWR, with contributions from the L&NWR, to other British ports for bunkering [8], besides supplying heavy industry, railway companies and house-coal markets.

Passenger traffic was increasing, aided by commuting developments focused on Cardiff and increasing popularity of 'day' trips, notably to markets, shopping centres and sporting events. In the weeks before August

1914 local newspapers contained numerous advertisements for special trains, e.g. *'GWR Earlier Holidays'* [9] advertising a range of trips especially to Bristol and Weston-Super-Mare, as well as Ascot Races. Also advertised were *'weekly excursions for a week or a fortnight'* to destinations including Devon and Cornwall resorts, London, Ireland and a range of places in north and eastern England, which ran almost every day in the week. August Bank holiday generated a range of excursions by the L&NWR from the Rhymney Valley, as well as 'period excursions' to mid and north Wales operated jointly by the TVR, RR, B&MR and Cambrian Railways *'by the direct route via Talyllyn'* [10]. Such activities reflect optimism on the part of the railway companies.

The performance of the companies named in the study area are summarised below :

Company	Year	Dividend Paid	Mineral Traffic (tons)	Passenger Traffic (numbers)
RR [11]	1908	7%	3,500,000	3,451,027
	1912	9%	5,787,249	3,594,924
B&MR [12]	1908	4%	Mineral tonnage up.	1907 'best year ever'.
	1911	4%	Increased	Increased.
	1913	4%	3,500,000	-
TVR	1908 [13]	4%	c 16,000,000	Receipts & train mileage slightly down.
	1913 [14]	4%	19,000,000	-
GWR [15]	1908	5¼%	-	-
	1913	6¼%	-	-
L&NWR [16]	1910	6⅝%	-	-
	1913	7%	-	-

Table 2 Performance figures relating to railway companies operating in study area, pre 1914.

Not all lines in the study area enjoyed the same level of prosperity. The RR was performing particularly well. Coal traffic mainly directed to Cardiff Docks was rising steadily, thanks to the new, large, efficient collieries in the Rhymney Valley [17]. Additionally, the RR carried a considerable amount of iron ore and steel products from Dowlais Iron and Steel works. To manage this increasing traffic more effectively and efficiently the RR pioneered introduction of telephone-based traffic control system [18], besides laying additional tracks alongside the existing main line. Rapid population growth in the 'new' settlements near the new pits, e.g. Bargoed, was generating more passenger traffic, consequently the RR was investing in new stations; Bargoed, 1900-10, Caerphilly doubled in size 1911-14 and its

Cardiff terminus was next on its agenda, besides introducing more powerful locomotives and new bogie carriages; the latter like the rest of the fleet, being fitted with electric lighting.

For several years prior to 1905 the B&MR declared no dividend, but it benefitted, too, from the new collieries in the Rhymney Valley. Coal traffic increased markedly during the Edwardian period, despite much being despatched to the less favoured Newport Docks or syphoned off by the Barry Railway. Like the RR, passenger traffic was growing, as was its locomotive fleet, but investment in new stations and carriages was minimal. In essence the Rhymney Valley section of the B&MR had become the railway's main 'bread winner' helping to provide hapless B&MR shareholders with a return for their patient support.

The TVR exercised minimal direct impact on the study area prior to 1914, just the branch line to Nelson. In the nineteenth century it had been a railway phenomenon making large profits transporting huge quantities of Rhondda and Aberdare coal to Cardiff and Penarth Docks, such that a dividend of 17½% was paid in 1882 [19]. This prosperity was constrained when the Barry Railway opened its integrated dock and railway system (1888), redirecting large quantities of Rhondda and Cynon Valley coal to its new docks. Table 2 shows the TVR was still carrying a prodigious amount of coal, but unlike the Rhymney Valley, both Rhondda and Cynon Valleys were seeing smaller, less efficient pits close, with little development of modern, large collieries to replace them. Passenger traffic was high (not particularly so on the Nelson branch), but as population in the TVR hinterland was beginning to decline, so too were passenger receipts.

The GWR Aberdare - Pontypool Road route was a significant artery for coal traffic destined for English markets [20], which traversed the study area's southern fringes. There is evidence traffic was declining [21], for in 1885 40 eastbound trains were timetabled, but by 1900 this had fallen to 29, with a further slight drop by 1913. Post 1900 this could be explained by the introduction of larger, more powerful locomotives [22], pulling heavier, but fewer trains. Passenger services were on a par with the local lines, but operated over longer distances, particularly to connect with routes to England.

The L&NWR had links with several railways on the study area fringes. In the north its Merthyr - Abergavenny route linked with the RR at Rhymney Bridge and B&MR in Dowlais and Merthyr. Both provided some traffic, but this, 'heads of the valley' route, constructed primarily to serve local iron works was, like the iron works, in decline. L&NWR running powers over the RR line to Cardiff proved useful and profitable, but powers did not cover coal traffic, except for a small amount carried to English destinations. The L&NWR did not provide passenger services over the RR, yet had operated 'through' coaches from Cardiff (RR) to Manchester and Liverpool via Rhymney Bridge, but by 1913 such services were limited to parcels carriages. The most productive L&NWR route linked Sirhowy Valley collieries with the Barry Railway, via the GWR from Pontllanfraith to Hengoed, joining the RR for Ystrad Mynach, whence the RR worked trains to Penrhos Junction [23] with the Barry Railway.

There were, nevertheless, dark clouds on the railways' horizon in 1914. Costs were rising, partly due to increased trade union action in securing pay increases, which could not be recouped by increasing fares or rates - these were controlled by governments determined to prevent railway monopolies holding traders to ransom! Trade union activity, as in the coal industry, was increasingly directed by younger, more radical leaders whose agendas were determined more by political ideology than work force interests. Although no one was aware at the time, south Wales' coal production peaked in 1913, beginning a decline which continued until the 1990s, whereupon rail traffic contracted in concert. Furthermore, there were ominous signs of competition for the railways, especially for passenger traffic, from bus services, especially those operated by local councils. [24]

Such was the situation at 11 p.m. on 4 August 1914.

B&MR No. 37 – chalk inscription 'The Baltic Fleet 1913'. To what does it refer? Royal Navy did not have a 'Baltic Fleet' in 1913 – the Russian and German navies did. Was it a trial run for Admiralty Coal Specials? Or were the south Wales coalfields supplying the Russian Fleet? (*TM Collection*)

The Impact of the War

1) Railway Executive Committee

War impacted on the railways within an hour of the declaration, for at 11.45 pm. a telegram was sent to 130 [25] railway companies, including those in the study area, informing them, that with immediate effect, they had been placed under Government control and should follow the directions of the Railway Executive Committee until the end of the emergency.

The REC was established in 1912, following the Agadir incident [26], under the terms of Section 16 of the Regulation of the Forces Act, 1871. '... *to control, on behalf of the Board of Trade, such railways as might be taken possession of in the name of His Majesty in the event of an emergency ...*' [27] However, the President of the BoT emphasized '*the railways were their own masters and that they were not to be nationalised or treated as a state system* [28].' This was re-iterated by Herbert Walker, REC chairman on 4 August to clarify matters for railway users: '... *control of the railways has been taken over by the Government for the purpose of ensuring that the railways, locomotives rolling stock and staff shall be used as one complete unit in the best interests of the State for the movement of troops, stores and food supplies.*' Continuing, he stated, '*staff on each railway will remain under the same control as heretofore and will receive their instructions through the same channels as in the past* [29].' In short, the REC, comprising eleven of the leading railway company general managers [30], controlled strategic direction, while delegating day to day operations to the railway companies.

Apart from the demands of the REC, an '*outstanding feature of the 1914-18 war was the freedom with which the Government delegated important branches of national work to the management of officers, seconded from the railway service*' [31]. One such officer, was E.A. Prosser, RR General Manager, appointed Assistant Director of Movement for the REC, in 1917 [32]. Soon after, Edgar Davies from the RR Stores Superintendent Office was appointed to the Railway Troops Depot in France [33].

The first actions of the REC were:

i) Frank Potter, GWR General Manager reported to his Directors, that '*mobilisation was ordered on the night of 4 August and pre-arranged programmes were at once put into operation* [34].' In Rhymney that night '*notices of the mobilisation of Reservists and Territorials was posted ... army reservists from the town returned on Tuesday and Wednesday to Scotland, Ireland and different parts of Wales, the farewell scenes at stations being touching. On Wednesday the 'G' Company of the Territorial Force left for service via Newport ...*'

being given a *'hearty send off at the B&MR station ...* [35]' This was followed by Lord Kitchener's appeal for more men leading to scenes including: *'Large number of men seen leaving the Old Castle (Caerphilly) town by every train. On Tuesday a large number left for Cardiff on the midday train, whilst another batch went up the valley.*[36]' Horses, too, were subject to urgent call-up: *'At the outbreak of World War I government officials came to the Brewery to take away the finest of their animals (already being replaced by motor lorries), loaded into horse boxes at Rhymney station (RR?) and later shipped to France for hauling heavy guns ... and never returned* [37].

ii) Apart from services to bring Bank Holiday-makers home, between 4 – 19 August, all excursion trains were suspended [38], as were *'some locals and others of lesser importance ... to make way for troop movements* [39].' Disruption of passenger services continued beyond that time, as suggested: *'All trains ran on the GWR and RR this week, with the exception of the early morning cars. ... public must be very watchful as only short notice is given of any curtailment* [40].'

This pattern continued throughout the war as indicated in 1915: *'No Easter Holiday excursions at customary cheap fares this year... 'normal' holiday services will not run and only ordinary tickets to be issued on severely restricted services. Purpose – keep lines clear for troop trains, goods trains and need to keep war factories functioning full time* [41].'

iii) The War Office demanded bridges and various points along the permanent way were to be watched, consequently *'all the GWR platelayers stationed at Aberdare have been called out on special duty (supplemented by men from Llanhilleth, Aberbeeg and Risca) and stationed at Quaker's Yard & Llancaiach.'* [42] Later, military protection was undertaken by the National Reserve under Brigadier General Grove [43].

Although the railway companies readily accepted REC directions, there were tensions. The greatest was compensation. The companies went to war in August 1914, without any agreement with the Government about payment, simply believing compensation would be paid. In September 1914 terms were agreed, based on the difference in net receipts for 1913 compared with those of 1914 etc., plus special compensation for all special services rendered to the Government. This agreement was 'modified' by the Government in February 1915, when the railway companies agreed to pay 25% of the War Bonus given to railway workers to counter higher living costs. In August 1915 the Government awarded allowances to companies for deferred maintenance and renewal. Such funding, plus increased costs beyond the companies' control, did not meet the true cost of outgoings.

A major source of increased costs was the aforementioned War Bonus payable by June 1915 to all grades and ages. REC and Trades Unions agreements increased the Bonus on several occasions subsequently, which in October 1916 the Government conceded could be regarded as a working expense. The Bonus was made available to the increasing number of women employees as from September 1916. Following a further increase, in October 1917, the War Bonus was converted into a War Wage, thus giving men the benefit of higher overtime and Sunday working pay and in March 1918 the REC/Government agreed to men receiving a week's paid annual leave. During 1918 War Wages were increased twice, in April and November, applicable to all railway workers, while in August the War Bonus was also increased, 4/- per week for over 18s and 2/- for under 18s [44].

In September 1918 the unions and Government agreed an increase in War Wages, plus the establishment of a joint committee to ascertain increases in the cost of living and devise a sliding scale of wages congruent with that. This was accepted by most NUR branches with reservations, apart from some in south Wales, thus those in the Newport area decided to strike as from Monday 23 September, stopping both passenger and goods services on the GWR Aberdare - Pontypool Road route and the L&NWR line from Merthyr to Abergavenny. Following a meeting at the Independent Labour Party Offices, Merthyr Branch joined the stoppage on Tuesday 24 September, halting services on the TVR, the B&MR and some on the RR, mainly north of Bargoed. At a meeting in Cardiff, NUR Secretary, Right Honourable J.H. Thomas, M.P. convinced the men that they should return to work, as they had no support from the population at large, including the miners, and had been labelled 'unpatriotic', especially as it was suggested in general railwaymen's wages were 120 % above that paid in 1914 – more than the increases in cost of living [45].

Though short lived, the strike disrupted travel and business severely. On Tuesday 24 September 5,000 miners were idle at New Tredegar, Elliot, Bargoed and Britannia collieries because of a lack of trucks. Food supplies, notably perishables like fish and milk, were badly affected, particularly as Bargoed and surrounding townships received 60 % of their milk supply by rail [46].

The railway companies were aggrieved the REC permitted wage increases, but prevented them increasing fares and freight rates to off-set these additional costs. Despite receiving monthly compensation payments on top of receipts, the railways claimed they could not cover these and other non REC related cost increases. The Government imposed a 50 % increase in passenger fares as from 1 January 1917 [47], in conjunction with reductions in services, mainly to deter unnecessary passenger travel, but it was of limited benefit to the railways themselves. In 1917 the TVR reported it earned £21,000 more due to increased fares, while passenger numbers had fallen by over 2 million [48]. Not until January 1920 did the BoT allow freight rates and passenger fares to rise commensurate with costs [49], but damage had been inflicted with significant consequences for the future financial health of the railway industry.

Another cause of tension was the REC demand for reductions in passenger travel by cutting services, increasing Railway Fare Duty [50] and removing certain ticketing arrangements. The latter exercised Pontlottyn Chamber of Commerce in 1915 when they asked other Rhymney Valley Chambers: *'to co-operate … to secure reinstatement of cheap market fares on the RR for Wednesdays and Thursdays'*, besides *'the provision of cheap 2nd class fares.'* [51] The RR General Manager responded, *'re-instatement of cheap fares on half-holidays, is "entirely out of the Company's hands, the regulation of the lines having been taken over by the Railway Executive since the beginning of the war"* [52].' Complaints did not cease as shown in the following letter: *'Bedlinog – population in 1911 4,820 and now almost 6,000 and is an important colliery & agricultural centre. Railway facilities most unsatisfactory. First train – 8.51 am. too late to connect with early GWR/RR/TVR trains. Last evening train 7.37 pm. Saturdays excepted. … Booking office inconvenient, etc* [53].'

Although, the war generally saw reductions in passenger train services, there were a few occasions when this was lifted temporarily. August Bank holiday was cancelled in 1916, nevertheless *'on the GWR passenger traffic just as great as on a 'normal' Bank Holiday weekend.'* [54] A year later, despite significant reductions in passenger services, it was reported: *'Big exodus of holiday-seekers seen last Saturday. Trains from early morn till a late hour packed. Journeys to Swansea, Carmarthen, Cardigan, Tenby, Aberystwyth and Porthcawl – latter never been so full on August Bank holiday. Numbers also went to Pontsarn & Vaynor* [55].'

Being blamed for short-comings, largely beyond their control, frustrated the railway companies. Besides cuts in services, the REC restricted capital expenditure, curtailing many planned improvements. An example was an issue raised by Bargoed and Caerphilly Chambers' of Trade: *'the Commercial Travellers Association stated it had appointed two representatives to form a joint deputation of Chambers of Trades, etc. to wait upon the General Manager of the RR, asking for better heating facilities in passenger coaches* [56].' After an exchange of fruitless correspondence, Caerphilly Chamber of Trade's end of year report (1915) suggested *'The heating of RR carriages was 'hung up'.'* [57] No sooner had the war ended, with the railways still under REC control [58], Caerphilly Council received a letter from Nelson Trades & Labour Council ... *'to take up the cause of the public in regard to the dirty state of RR carriages, and their lack of warmth and comfort. ... the Council had already written to the General Manager of the RR Co. ... a reply had been received to the effect that the carriages were regularly swept, but that passengers put their feet on the seats. In regard to heating the carriages it had not been possible to do anything during the war, but the matter is now under consideration* [59]*,'* as it had been in 1914.

Such issues created a negative public attitude towards railway operations and management as exemplified in an article written by 'Recorder': *'Whatever may be the discontent of many of the public with the arrangements of the RR Co, and there have been and still are, complaints, accompanied with anger, the faults are not with the rank and file of the officials which one meets along the line. The RR Co. has had some splendid men on its staff; faithful, honest and courteous servants; and such servants make up for many of the shortcomings on the part of the shareholders and directors* [60]*.'* Furthermore, a Caerphilly councillor's retort to RR and TVR opposition to a Bill to establish a Council operated bus service, sums-up the attitude: *'the railway service had been so inadequate that the RR had been approached on several occasions, but the management pleaded that their first duty was to get the coal down (to the ports)* [61]*.'*

In 1917, the War Office requested the urgent despatch of locomotives to France, whereupon the GWR responded by lending 62 'Dean Goods' tender locomotives [62], plus 11 newly built mixed traffic tender locomotives [63]. To compensate for this 'loss' of motive power the GWR adjusted its locomotive allocations, including: *'...all six GWR locos departed from Caeharris to Pontypool Road and Aberdare – shortage of engines following despatch of engines to France. Entire work devolved onto RR Co* [64]*.'* This put pressure on the RR, especially as delivery of new locomotives ordered in 1914 was slow, consequently the RR applied to the GWR for a loan of three engines [65]. In the meantime, the increasing numbers of Admiralty Specials and re-organisation of coal distribution led to the GWR identifying a need for 24 new locomotives, which they were allowed to construct in early 1918 [66].

It is little wonder that at a B&MR Board meeting it was commented that *'(we) would be glad to see Government agreement at an end – could develop railway more quickly ourselves* [67]*.'* Similar views were implied at a TVR Board meeting *'railways still under government control, with the REC directing operations of entire railway system of the country* [68]*.'*

2) Admiralty Special Coal Trains – 'Jellicoe Specials'

It was as early as the 1840s that the Royal Navy, experimenting with steam ships, designated south Wales Dry Steam Coal as the favoured source of fuel for its ships. Despite politicking by other coalfield interests, the RN was resolute in favouring steam coal from the Rhondda and Cynon Valleys for its capital ships and by the turn of the twentieth century an Official Admiralty List of supplying colliery companies had been compiled, designating two grades:

i)   Best or Premier Grade having a carbon content of over 83.4 % for use in large fighting ships and escorts in the Grand Fleet.

ii) Second Grade with a carbon content of over 77.2 % used in smaller vessels, including convoy escort ships, some destroyers and supply ships. [69]

By 1914 most of the 'best' coal came from the Rhondda and Cynon Valleys, but collieries in the study area on the Admiralty list included (Table 3):

Colliery Company	Colliery	Railway Co. serving	Location	Production Large Coal 1914 (tons)	Production Large Coal 1917 (tons)	Best / Second Grade
G.K.&N. (Dowlais)	Fochriw	RR/GWR/ B&MR	Fochriw	211,322	199,976	Best
	Bedlinog	RR/GWR	Bedlinog	217,092	182,203	Best
Ocean	Deep Navigation	GWR/RR	Treharris	n/a	n/a	Best
Powell Duffryn	Penallta	RR	Ystrad Mynach	294,787	310,526	Second
	New Tredegar	RR/B&MR	New Tredegar	114,786	80,271	Best
	Bargoed	RR/B&MR	Bargoed	184,554	112,617	Second
	Elliot	RR/B&MR	New Tredegar	254,519	195,639	Second
	Britannia	B&MR/RR	Pengam	16,034*	101,166	Second
Rhymney Coal & Iron Co.	Groesfaen	RR	Nr Bargoed	217,092	143,650	Second
	Rhymney Merthyr	RR	Pontlottyn	143,465	110,315	Best
Tredegar Coal & Iron Co.	McLaren Merthyr	B&MR (Barry Rly.)	Abertysswg	n/a	n/a	Second

*Britannia did not start producing coal until mid-1914.

Sources: Turton, K. Admiralty Coal Traffic During the First World War, Part 1, Railway Archive Issue 19, June 2008 and Merthyr Express 27/03/1915.

Table 3 – Collieries in Study area on Admiralty List.

Prior to August 1914, RN ships coaled either at south Wales ports, or at naval ports, mostly on the south and east coasts, to which coal was transported by ship from south Wales ports. The Agadir Incident (1911) alerted the Admiralty to the possibility of conflict, whereupon a thorough review of coal transport needs was undertaken. Appreciating that shipping coal to the East Coast naval bases could be vulnerable to attack, the GWR was involved in a planning role for rail transport from south Wales as early as 1911. Indeed, the Times reported a trial run from south Wales to Scotland [70], highlighting many potential problems of such an operation and forming the basis of a GWR 'Special Notice' of January 1912. Complicating matters in the weeks prior to the war's declaration, the Grand Fleet was moved to bases in Scotland, including Rosyth and Invergordon, with Scapa Flow in the Orkney Islands being the principal anchorage. Over the course of the war, as table 4 shows south Wales coal was despatched by rail to a number of ports, especially in Scotland, from where it was loaded into ships and carried to the Grand Fleet's bases [71].

Destination Port	Tons of coal delivered
Grangemouth	2,346,879
Immingham	851,890
Glasgow	717,459
Tyne ports	488,008
Burntisland	309,290
Leith	482,161
Hull	13,681
Other East Coast Ports	59,607
Southampton	283,353
Birkenhead	302,522
Gosport	213,224
Devonport	109,645
Holyhead	76,265
Thames	316,721
Chatham	36,201

Source: Pratt, E.A. 'War Record of the GWR', London, 1921.

Table 4 – Ports to which Admiralty Special Coal Trains worked, 1914-19.

A major problem emerging during the trial, and that continued throughout the war, was the availability of suitable coal wagons. Through its agents at Cardiff, William Mathwin & Sons, the Admiralty initially hired 4,000 wagons from H. G. Lewis & Co. Ltd., of Cardiff. These were of ten or twelve ton capacity with end-doors for unloading, usually used on short distance trains from the Valleys to the docks. However, the general condition of private owner coal wagons was moderate at best, as indicated in RR reports of accidents – 8 incidents relating to such wagons were reported within the study area in 1914 and 9 in 1915, mostly involving broken couplings or drawbars (reported as being 'flawed') [72], therefore, workings were hampered by frequent breakdowns, need for regular inspections and slow operating speeds – 25 mph maximum. Nevertheless they persevered and as sea lanes became more hazardous more wagons had to be obtained. Ultimately about 16,000 were hired.

The GWR arrangements for these special trains or 'Jellicoe Specials' [73] specified Pontypool Road as the main assembly and starting point. Trains were specially labelled, had their own special signal box bell code, operating instructions and locomotives – initially the GWR 26xx class was specified between Pontypool Road and Warrington hauling 34 loaded wagons, but later, more powerful 28xx class were allocated, capable of hauling up to 50 loaded wagons.

Although Pontypool Road was the main concentration point for loaded coal wagons, Quaker's Yard, a junction between the TVR and GWR Aberdare - Pontypool Road line, was an important exchange point for Rhondda and Cynon Valleys coal. As the war progressed a slightly easier, but longer, route via Pontypridd (TVR), Penrhos in Caerphilly (Alexander Dock Railway), Ystrad Mynach (RR) and Nelson (GWR) was also used. Though not confirmed by available evidence, it is likely Admiralty coal from study area collieries would have also been worked to Quaker's Yard, but there were other interchange points on the GWR route e.g. Ffaldcaiach (GWR/RR Joint), Nelson (RR), Hengoed (RR) and Maesycwmmer (B&MR). Indeed, from the latter the GWR had two daily timetabled workings from Pontypool Road to Rhymney (B&MR), plus a 'conditional' working to New Tredegar, with a timetable reference to Admiralty coal or empties workings to '*P.D. Company's pits*' [74]. At Quaker's Yard loaded wagons were assembled into trains and worked to Pontypool Road, by one of three routes:

i) Quaker's Yard – Crumlin – Pontypool Road.

ii) Quaker's Yard – Hengoed – Bird in Hand Junction (Sirhowy Valley line) – Newport – Maindee – Pontypool Road.

iii) Quaker's Yard – Ystrad Mynach – Caerphilly – Bassaleg – Newport – Maindee – Pontypool Road.

Adding these special trains to an already busy route; the Quaker's Yard - Pontllanfraith line, made it one of the busiest in south Wales, if not the whole UK, during the war years. As the war progressed the number of Admiralty Specials generally increased, from 82 in January 1915 to 611 in March 1918, while in November 1918 on one day nearly 40 extra trains departed from Quaker's Yard [75].

Unusually, the local press commented: '*Great increase in coal traffic passing Quaker's Yard station during past few weeks. GWR taxed to cope. One result – short notice stoppage of entire rail motor service Aberdare – Quaker's Yard* [76].' It was reported to the GWR Board that the siding accommodation at Quaker's Yard was '*adequate for only 289 wagons, but in 13 days ending 24/11/1917 the number exchanged was 11,054, an average of 850 per day. The accommodation was not designed for such traffic – standing wagons are often kept on running lines. More facilities are required to cope with the movement of traffic.*' In spring 1918 the GWR secured '*authority from War Office for additional work to be undertaken immediately:*

- *Quaker's Yard – Extension of 2 sidings - £1,619.*
- *Nelson & Llancaiach – Up goods running loop; Additional sidings to hold 328 wagons; shunting spur; new signal box – cost £14,520.*
- *Pontypool Road – 3 additional sidings; 2 cripple sidings - £5,950* [77].'

Aerial view of Nelson. At the top of the photograph are the sidings completed in autumn 1918, built by the GWR/RR to supplement the limited amount of accommodation at Quaker's Yard. (*TM Collection*)

Progress was noted in the press: '*GWR and RR will shortly commence new sidings between Nelson & Penallta Jct, a work rendered necessary by the large amount of war traffic* [78]. Later it was reported: '*A large number of our local discharged soldiers and sailors are working on the new GWR sidings between Nelson and Penallta Junction* [79],' followed by: '*Great progress being made with new GWR sidings ... a new signal box has been erected in connection therewith, near the Powell's Works crossing* [80].' Finally: '*New GWR sidings at Nelson & Llancaiach comprising seven* distinct lines are now practically completed. *The new sidings will give facilities for the accommodation of a large amount of rolling stock* [81].' These sidings remained *in situ*, but underutilised, until 1965, while the signal box closed in 1932 [82].

By early 1918 GWR routes were at saturation point, consequently less busy alternatives were employed: *'To ease the traffic on the main line, four trains a day were worked from south Wales pits via Pontsticill to Talyllyn by the B&MR, where the Cambrian Railways took over ...'*. The trains *'were double headed with two engines attached behind to assist to Torpantau* [83].' Although some trains originated in Merthyr, others started from the Rhymney Valley [84], with most destined for Birkenhead. Overall, the B&MR worked 250 trains carrying about 100,000 tons of coal.

The first 'Jellicoe Special' departed Pontypool Road at 12.35 pm. on 27 August 1914 and between then and 31 December 1918 a further 13,630 specials were run, carrying about 6½ million tons of coal. In addition, 8,161 return empties specials were run [85]. This was an enormous and successful logistical exercise *'executed with nothing less than heroic efficiency by an undermanned and underequipped privately owned railway system. Coupled with this was the almost legendary, hopelessly unrecognised and under-valued feats of its employees ...* [86].' The last Admiralty coal train ran in March 1919.

3) Coal Traffic – General

'Moving the coal' spurred construction of many local railways, thus the war had both indirect and direct effects on coal traffic. Pre-war traffic flows were maintained in the early years of the war, but changes were taking place progressively altering the markets for coal and its movements.

On the Thursday preceding the declaration of war, *'every colliery on Admiralty list notified their entire output of dry steam coal was to be reserved. Large fleet of colliers made available (ships carrying coal for Russian, Greek, Italian, Austrian and other navies stopped) and other vessels in dock taken over by authorities. Agents required ships for the Admiralty to be loaded day/night through the Bank Holiday weekend – coal trimmers and railwaymen responded loyally, but Welsh miners did not – leaders deemed order not that urgent and condemned Government for interference in foreign war* [87].' By this action the Government had closed, permanently as it turned out, a number of major markets to south Wales coal. Coal not subject to Admiralty contract could be exported, but as an increasing number of coal carrying ships were sequestered for coal transport for the Fleet, serving overseas markets became more difficult. When sinkings of colliers [88] made shipping too hazardous, more markets were lost. Partly compensating for these export losses was an increase in demand for south Wales coal in the home market which could be reached by rail, thus traffic flows began to change from 'pit to port' to that of a west – east flow.

Rail transport of coal

Reference above to Welsh miners' action proved a portent of trouble to come. In summer 1916 crisis point was reached, for notwithstanding the south Wales miners' demand for a 15% wage increase being conceded in June [89], *'a special conference of the 'Fed' decided to take two days holiday ... (August Bank Holiday)'* despite the *'Government ordering owners to keep pits open ready for work on those two days* [90].' Belatedly bonuses were offered to maintain production, nevertheless reversal of the decision brought expressions of *'profound relief ... that the 'unpatriotic resolution' of the conference ... to stop work for two days, which experience has taught us ... would have meant the paralysis of a whole week's work at the collieries. ... ... has saved its good name amongst its fellow countrymen ... a scandalous exhibition of recklessness in the hour of the nation's peril. We hope we have seen the last of these acts on the part the Fed in hostility to the Government. ... hope that henceforward the miners will remember that while we are engaged in a war for our national existence no sacrifice is too great to be made in support of the common weal* [91].' A prescient writer, using the pseudonym 'Percy' warned: *'the nationalism (sic) of the railways for the period of the war has been brought about and nationalisation of the collieries permanently is only a step further. From many points of view it is undesirable, but if the masters insist on getting huge profits and the men insist upon huge wages and refuse to work when the Nation calls for coal, then neither can complain if the Government steps in* [92].' In November 1916, the BoT, using the Defence of the Realm Act, took control of the Welsh coalfield when another pay claim *'threatened to plunge coal field into another stoppage ... collieries instructed to carry on ...*[93].' An uneasy peace reigned as the 'Fed' felt it had won the political argument ... until 1921.

In September 1917 the Controller of Mines [94] reorganised coal transport, entailing consumers to obtain their coal supplies from the nearest coal producing centre. South Wales supplies were directed to centres of increasing demand in the south west and London and south east. For the GWR this caused problems:

- GWR locomotives operating in the Midlands could not be supplied with Welsh coal, for which they had been designed.

- Additional traffic placed on already congested routes – need for more sidings.

- 'Coal supplies for London – regular booked additional trains require 17 extra engines [95].'

The biggest difficulty affecting both mines and railways was shortage of wagons, a result of a general undersupply of wagons, the need to return empty wagons to originating collieries and wagons detained unnecessarily for storage (demurrage) – latter a statutory offence in 1917 [96]. Although export and import traffic to/from ports was reduced this was off-set by increases in railway usage, e.g. domestic timber, iron and steel raw and finished materials, munitions and coal, notably the 'Admiralty Specials' [97]. One significant 'new' local demand reported in 1917 and falling on the RR, was: *'Iron ore unloaded at Cyfarthfa works – furnaces soon to be fired [98].'* Almost the 'last straw' was the War Office call for 20,000 wagons to be sent abroad [99].

The shortage problem was discussed at a meeting in March 1916, *'GWR, L&NWR, Midland, L&Y, NER – preparing scheme for 'common user' for open goods wagons [100].'* This was reported to be 'working satisfactorily' in April 1916 and extended in 1917 to 'pool' all railway company owned wagons. However, the vast majority of coal traffic was handled in 'private owner' wagons, whose work was customarily limited to workings between owning collieries and docks or customer, necessitating empty return workings and a lot of additional shunting. Despite the advantages of pooling these wagons, such was the complexity of the notion, the REC demurred from so doing. Nevertheless, shortages increased, consequently in an *'Order in Council [101], BoT 16/03/17 – Railway Companies given power to take possession of privately owned wagons and use them for loaded return journey [102].'* This helped, but did not prevent collieries being idle for 'want of trucks' or because of 'stop trucks', e.g. October 1917-January 1918 – Fochriw and Penallta idle on at least three occasions [103].

Labour shortages

Such was the depth of patriotic fervour on the outbreak of war that many miners flocked to the army recruiting offices. The outflow soon became a problem, as the Rhymney Iron Company reported in 1915: *'difficulty in securing labour, work at many pits underground at standstill since August 1914. Production down – output 1914-15 1,103,694 tons (1913-14 1,304,297 tons) – due to labour shortage. 20% of company work force joined colours. Costs of production increased [104].'* The Powell Duffryn Steam Coal Company reported in April 1915 1,415 men had 'joined the colours', a number increasing by November 1918 to 6,407 [105] leading to a decline in overall production, which in the study area mainly affected the older pits (see Table 3 above). Continuing fall in production caused concern, as exemplified by the following report of 1918: *'Since Whit-Monday the Navy League carried out a successful campaign and addressed many large and patriotic audiences in Rhymney Valley etc. Object – to appeal to miners to produce as much coal as possible for the Navy; to combat any pacifist element at work and generally preserve national unity and help win war* [106].'

The lure of the recruiting office caused labour shortages for railway companies too, such that concerns raised by the REC in 1915 led to General Kitchener requesting the companies to estimate *'minimum number of men required for the efficient working of the railways – also ascertain number of men 18-45 who could be replaced by youths under 18, men over 45 or women* [107].' In 1918 the RR General Manager reported: *'399 employees joined HM services during the war. 29 discharged, 17 resumed work with RR and 12 into other employment. 31 killed in action, 45 wounded in action, 5 P.O.W., 4 received decorations*[108].' The B&MR Board reported in 1916: *'63 men joined colours and nine clerical staff – 2 others killed and 3 PoW.'* As a result, the company was: *'Short of hands – had to do best we could*[109].' Contemporaneously, the TVR Board reported: *'800 have joined the colours. Suitable provision made for wives, families and other dependents during their absence* [110].' That similar provisions were made by the RR is implied in references to the Board in 1915*: 'Mr Prosser reported on conversations with Mr Beasley (TVR) about allowances for clerks who have joined colours,'* and *'… to dependents of unmarried employees … and received instructions* [111].'

A WELSH STATIONMISTRESS.

Miss Lidster, daughter of Chief Inspector Lidster, of the Great Western Railway, Pontypool, began duty yesterday morning as stationmistress at Troedyrhiew Halt, on the joint Great Western and Rhymney Railway, near Merthyr. This is the first woman official to act in such a capacity in South Wales.

Another woman is being appointed to take charge of Trelewis Junction, their predecessors in each case having joined the Army.

The dining cars on G.W.R. trains to South Wales are now in charge of female attendants.

Cambrian Daily Leader 20th April 1915

Awareness of the long working hours caused by the shortage of railwaymen contributed to the Prime Minister's (Lloyd George) conceding the principle of an 'eight hour day' to railwaymen. The local press reported: *'The public should know that railwaymen's hours … have been the longest of any class of labour in the country – ten hours a day … the mental strain upon*

165

drivers, firemen and signalmen … is exhausting when kept upon the stretch for ten hours consecutively [112].' There is a record of a B&MR engine driver in 1916 working shifts in excess of eleven hours on several occasions during his six day working week – he died of a heart attack that year [113].

Inflation

Inevitably, wartime shortages led to price inflation affecting all individuals and organisations e.g. the local press reported in 1915 the price of good quality coal had increased since August 1914, from 29/6d to 40/- per ton[114]. For the railway companies price increases added considerably to their working costs, as exemplified below in relation to the RR:

Date	Total Coal ordered (tons)	Average cost per ton
12/1914	33,600	16/7d
11/1917	40,800	29/8d (final 1918 cost)

Source: RR Minutes of Directors' Meetings 1914-18.

Table 5 – rising cost of locomotive coal for RR, 1914-18.

To assist the railway companies the Coal Controller suggested, through the REC, that patent fuel could be substituted for large coal. Soon after the RR Board reported: '*Mr Prosser authorised to use patent fuel in the ratio of one third patent fuel to two thirds large coal* [115].' Anecdotal evidence suggests it was not a successful experiment.

The RR and other railway companies had to cope with a range of cost increases e.g.:

Dates	Item	Increased cost
07/1915	Fencing	Price increased in past year.
03/1916 to 12/1918	Telegraph Lines contract	5% increase – duration of war. Further increase requested – 10/1916. Further increase requested – 02/1918. 8.5% increase – 07/1918. 2 further increases by 12/1918.
03/1916.	Costs of locomotives	£200 extra per locomotive demanded on delivery (ordered 12/1914).
10/1915 to 04/1918	Cost of new locomotive boilers for 'K' class	1915 - £820 each. 1918 - £1,295.

Source: RR Minutes of Directors' Meetings 1914-18.

Table 6 – exemplars of inflation in essential items required by RR, 1914-18[116].

As intimated previously, despite these increased costs, neither the RR, nor other railway companies could adjust fares and rates to reflect this, thus economies had to be made in the service offered. However, some commented adversely about the retention of relatively high dividends to shareholders, an argument countered by the railway companies to the effect that the shareholders owned the company and they were legally bound to do so.

Miscellaneous impacts

Even within the study area other events impacted upon the railways, but the war aggravated them. As the war progressed, food shortages increased, mainly resulting from the country's dependency on imported food, carried in ships vulnerable to attack by German 'U' boats and surface raiders. In 1916 the *'GWR offered staff land alongside allotments at an annual rent of 3d and any other uncultivated land offered to gardeners for free* [117].' This was not a new idea: *'What Mr Prothero of the Board of Agriculture is advocating as regards allotments has been done by the railwaymen of Quaker's Yard for 30 years, as travellers know, with the result they can now view with equanimity the high price of potatoes* [118].' Earlier that year in Nelson, it was reported *'several railwaymen now hold plots of ground on the boggy land near the station... rendered possible by ploughing and draining. The sides of the station approach are also being cultivated this year* [119].' This spurred on others to grow more food in gardens and on newly created allotments.

Exceptional weather events are not unique to wartime, but a few such events added to the railways' burdens. The most dramatic was the *'terrific blizzard'* experienced overnight on Monday 27 and Tuesday 28 March 1916. The impact was considerable: *'Tuesday morning no work at collieries nor iron works – continued into Wednesday. Fochriw and Bedlinog did not resume working until Thursday night. Travelling could not be done for either days. B&MR shed at Dowlais blown down. Rail traffic suspended all day Tuesday on all lines coming to Dowlais – RR/LNWR/B&MR.'* Furthermore *'Snow drifts at Fochriw. Line not cleared for traffic till Friday 31 March. 9.50 pm. Rhymney – Newport derailed at New Tredegar. Goods loco derailed at Cwmsyfiog. GWR loco snowed up at Elliot Colliery. Rhymney branch cleared of snow by 10 pm. on Tuesday 28 March* [120]. Under the heading 'gale and heavy snow' the RR Board were informed of damage done to telegraph poles and wires cost £16,000 to repair [121].

Another 'blizzard' was reported in 1918 when Dowlais and Nelson reportedly had several inches of snow. However, damage to telegraph lines etc. was *'not as bad as the blizzard of 1916* [122]. Other weather references were limited to heavy rain seriously damaging crops in south Wales in

August 1917 [123], a month considered the wettest *'within memory'* [124]. These events seem to have had little impact on the railways, but in 1915 the B&MR suffered a recurrence of landslides, often associated with particularly wet weather, impeding traffic near New Tredegar colliery, necessitating purchase of a steam navvy to assist debris clearance [125].

Accidents also impact on railway operations, but during the war years, while there were accidents in the study area, none could be firmly ascribed to wartime working conditions and only one involved a passenger train. Several accidents were 'runaways' where a train crew lost control of a heavily laden goods train travelling down a steep gradient. Two were reported, one in 1917, the other 1918, on the GWR/RR Joint line between Cwmbargoed and Ffaldcaiach [126], while a third occurred in 1915 on the B&MR/RR line between Fochriw and Bargoed [127]. There were two reported derailments, both on the GWR route in 1916, involving a *'big GWR side tank engine'* at Quaker's Yard [128] and *'the tender of a big GWR engine and two wagons derailed'*, near Treharris. The line was cleared within two hours by a breakdown gang sent from Aberdare [129]. Three incidents were caused by defective wagons, two on the Dowlais – Ffaldcaiach line in 1915 and 1918; the former resulting in the death of an engine driver whose locomotive ran into the detached wagons [130], while the latter resulted in a wagon-load of rails being scattered over the line [131]. The third, near Treharris (GWR) involved a RR mineral train, on which a loaded wagon's axle broke wrecking the wagon and track. *'Much delay resulted, as the down line had to be worked as a 'single line' and the breakdown gang had to be sent for from Aberdare* [132].*'* Three collisions occurred because signalmen 'forgot' stationary trains. The first, at Hengoed (RR) in 1915 involved two goods trains [133], while the second, minor incident, was at Dowlais [134]. A third in January 1917, resulted from a goods train being allowed to run on the 'wrong' line, so colliding with a RR 'motor train' at Gibbons Crossing, Tiryberth, injuring seventeen passengers and three enginemen [135]. Fortunately, none of these events delayed traffic for longer than a day or so, thus war traffic was not unduly incommoded.

Conclusions

There is little doubt the Great War had a great impact on Britain's railways generally, as well as those in the study area. The principal effect on the privately owned railways was the imposition of Government control for seven years (relinquished after the Railways Act 1921 was passed) whereby the strategic planning aspects of railway management were placed with the REC. No longer could the companies, through their Boards of Directors, plan and budget for their future. Some talk of the *'success of the quasi-nationalised framework of the Railway Executive ...'* [136], a questionable assertion as wartime expediency meant the REC took little account of the financial effects of their actions. Operational costs were allowed to rise, e.g. war wages, eight hour day, cost of coal and essential materials, while ignoring requests from the railways to raise fares and freight rates to take account of such increases and concomitant inflation. Pratt intimated that much war traffic was *'carried for 'free' by railway companies under terms of Government guarantee* [137],' the latter being enshrined in the promised compensation. In 1919-20 it was estimated the value of these services was £29 million more than the compensation received, causing the Railway Gazette to suggest the *'Government made an advantageous 'bargain' in 1914* [138].'

The upheaval caused by 4½ years of war left the railways in a very run-down condition, railway workers were exhausted and substantial investment was needed to restore pre-war standards, but being financially compromised, many were unable to cope with post war recovery. It is little wonder there were complaints about dirty carriages, slow unpunctual services and the railways apparent tardiness in returning services to normal or even better than 'normal'.

Despite the quantity of coal carried for the Admiralty, coal production declined, never to recover, as many former export markets for coal were lost. The unkindest loss followed the signing of the Treaty of Versailles in 1919, whereby France, a major user of south Wales coal, was provided with German coal in reparation for war damages. Technological change also played a part, with the conversion of the RN fleet to oil fuel, which commenced in 1911 accelerated post war, being spurred by the British Government's purchase of a controlling interest in the Anglo Persian Oil Company (later BP) in 1914 [139]. Following the RN lead, British merchant shipping lines also began to convert ships to oil burning, thus reducing the steam coal market further. While this impacted initially on the coal companies, the railways also suffered a significant loss of traffic, exacerbated by the simultaneous decline in the south Wales iron and steel industry.

For a while passenger traffic remained fairly buoyant as many wartime cuts in service were restored, though some cuts remained permanent, e.g. the loss of Sunday passenger services on the Pontypool Road – Aberdare line[140]. Nevertheless, the railway companies were under increasing attack for the quality of services and rolling stock. As economic decline set-in, aggravated by industrial disputes, passenger receipts also declined.

Stimulated by wartime restrictions in railway services, criticism from local politicians and sharp post war increases in freight rates, road transport emerged as a serious competitor. Despite the precipitous departure of South Wales Motor Transport's buses from the Rhymney Valley in 1917 [141] local councils were keen to promote Bills for additional licenses for omnibus services, which for ideological reasons they wished to operate and control themselves [142]. In addition, even during the war charabanc outings were operated *in lieu* of railway excursions [143], but immediately post war such outings gained enormously in popularity [144].

Even certain types of freight transport became susceptible to road competition, as discharged soldiers trained in the use and maintenance of lorries purchased ex-Army vehicles cheaply and set-up as hauliers, free from any of the constraints relating to freight carriage and rates imposed on the railways. Thus more traffic was lost to rail.

Overall, despite serving the country honourably in its 'hour of need' the war brought loss of traffic, a sharp deterioration in rail infrastructure, a reduction in public goodwill and for many, near and inescapable financial ruin, which effectively saw the beginning of the end of the era of railway domination of transport in the UK and the study area. In short, though the railways had helped win the war, they 'lost' in the peace.

For references see pages 173 - 174

GWR No. 2805 '28xx' class 2-8-0 at Aberdare shed, 1930s. These locomotives, introduced from 1903, were the mainstay of the Admiralty Coal Specials from Pontypool Road, but several were involved in coal workings from Aberdare throughout the war, including 2805. (*TM Collection*)

Armistice, Peace and Memorial

Received instructions from Chief Education Official that Glamorgan Education Committee granted 13, 14 and 15 November as holidays in celebration of the signing of the Armistice.

(Extract from a local school log book 1918)

While local schoolchildren enjoyed an Armistice holiday, residents in communities across Gelligaer Urban District decorated their homes with flags and bunting, formed jubilant processions behind their village Band and attended end-of-war thanksgiving services in, among other local places of worship, Fochriw's St. Mary's Church and Ebenezer Welsh Congregational Chapel in Trelewis.

The following notes provide some insight into what local people read in the local press in the final weeks of 1918 as discharged service personnel started to return home and people readjusted:

- In December 1918, Merthyr Furnishing Company's half page advertisement in *Merthyr Express* urged readers to buy easy chairs and bedding to create homely conditions for returning heroes to rest and relax. Sadly, not all heroes returned home.

- Through the columns of *Merthyr Express* December 21 1918, Frank Harrison, Jeweller and Optician of Hanbury Road, Bargoed, informed his customers that he was able to carry out sight tests in person after returning from eighteen months in the colours during which time his wife had seen to the business.

- A report in *Merthyr Pioneer* on December 21 1918 shows that Gelligaer Education Committee was intent on renewing its school-building programme in anticipation of the growth of the school populations in Bargoed, as family men like Albert Joseph Gerrish moved in when the new *1,000 houses of the "Great Peace"* were built, and Trelewis, where houses would be built for incomers working in the new sinkings in the area.

- 1918's final issue of *Merthyr Express* carried a report on a Cymmrodorion Society meeting in Nazareth Schoolroom, Pontlottyn, when members heard a lecture on Hedd Wyn.

While the signing of the Armistice was celebrated in November 1918, the Peace was not celebrated until July 1919, when, in common with communities countrywide, people across Gelligaer Urban District enjoyed sports, teas, carnivals and concerts. The illustration inside the back cover of this volume (reproduced from a copy held in Holy Trinity Church, Ystrad Mynach) shows the front page of *Celebrations of Peace* held in the grounds

171

of Ystrad Fawr.

Ystrad Fawr was home to Col. and Mrs Lindsay, parents who lost three sons in the conflict. Their oldest son, George Walter Thomas Lindsay, a Captain in Royal Flying Corps, died, June 26 1917, aged 26, and was buried in the family vault in Holy Trinity Churchyard, Ystrad Mynach. His two younger brothers were killed in action in late March 1918: Lieutenant Archibald Thurston Thomas Lindsay, was only 20 years old when he fell, March 26 1918, while Major Claud Frederic Thomas Lindsay, was 26 when he lost his life March 31 1918. The former was buried in Foncquevillers Military Cemetery, Pas de Calais, while the latter was buried near the middle of Hailles Communal Cemetery, Somme.

Their names are listed among those of other local casualties on Hengoed and Ystrad Mynach war memorial, unveiled by Col. Lindsay in a ceremony in 1927. Today that war memorial stands, in the grounds of Ysbyty Ystrad Fawr, just yards from their former home. They are also commemorated on a memorial on the wall of Church of St. John The Divine, Cwmbach Llechryd, Radnorshire, a church built at the expense of Miss Clara Thomas of Pencerrig, who, like their mother, was great granddaughter of Thomas Thomas of Llanbradach (1735-1807).

Note: There is further information about these two memorials on the following websites:

www.gelligaerhistoricalsociety.co.uk/index.php/ystrad-mynach-ww1

www.roll-of-honour.com/Radnorshire/CwmbachLlechryd.html

What Gwenllian Lewis and Glyn Williams, and so many other local people, whether or not they are named in this volume, saw and did during the war had a profound influence not just on their thinking but also on post-war developments in the local area, Britain and the wider world. While Lawrence Louis Sidney Cook and Austin P. Cunningham, typical of so many of their contemporaries, would not discuss their war time experiences with their families, an ever-growing range of sources, many readily-accessible on the internet, has enabled their grandchildren to uncover so much of that experience.

The lives of men, women and children who celebrated the Armistice and the Peace and who honoured the fallen had been changed by the war, and the end of hostilities did not witness return to the pre-August 4 1914 social, economic and political order.

References for The Impact of the Great War on the railways of Gelligaer Parish and adjoining areas by Terry McCarthy

1. For a more detailed synopsis of these lines please refer to: McCarthy, T.J. 'Impact of Railway Development on the Parish of Gelligaer', Gelligaer Vol. XVIII, Journal of Gelligaer Historical Society, 2010.
2. Dates of Acts of Incorporation.
3. The full title of the railway, usually abbreviated to Brecon & Merthyr Railway.
4. L&NWR was a company formed by amalgamation of the London & Birmingham (1830), Grand Junction (1830) and Liverpool & Manchester (1825) Railways.
5. There was another GWR & RR Joint line from Quaker's Yard to Merthyr built in 1886.
6. Legally entitled 'running powers'.
7. Barry Railway (1884) operated between Barry Docks and Rhondda, with a branch to the RR at Penrhos - extended to cross Rhymney Valley at Llanbradach in 1905 – planned an independent line to Abertysswg (contract awarded by Tredegar Iron & Coal Co.) but were 'bought off' by the B&MR and allowed to use their tracks, the cost of doubling of which secured a significant BR contribution.
8. Coal for steam ship bunkers – prior to World War I the vast majority of ships burned coal to raise steam, south Wales dry steam coal being the fuel of choice.
9. Merthyr Express 10/06/1914.
10. Merthyr Express 25/07/1914.
11. 1908 Railway Times. 1912 from RAIL 583/15.
12. Figures 1908/11 from Railway Times. 1913 – Barrie, D.S.M. revised Kidner, R.W. 'The Brecon & Merthyr Railway,' Oxford, 1991.
13. Merthyr Express 13/08/1910.
14. Merthyr Express 05/02/1916.
15. Figures from MacDermot, E.T. revised Clinker, C.R., 'History of the Great Western Railway Volume II 1863-1921,' London, 1964. No figures relating to individual lines in the study area seem to exist.
16. Figures from Nock, O.S., 'The London & North Western Railway,' London, 1960. No figures relating to individual lines in the study area seem to exist.
17. Elliot, Bargoed, Britannia, Penallta and Groesfaen.
18. 'Traffic Control on the Rhymney Railway.' The Railway Magazine, Vol. XXXII January to June 1913, London.
19. Barrie, D.S. 'The Taff Vale Railway,' Tanglewood, Surrey, 1950.
20. Destinations included Southampton, Birkenhead and Plymouth Docks, locomotive coal for London and industrial coal for the West Midlands via Oxford.
21. Jones, G.B. & Dunstone, D. 'The Vale of Neath Line', Llandysul, 1996.
22. Some of the UK's most powerful goods locomotives, built at Swindon from 1903 were allocated to this route and were still operating on it when it closed in 1964.
23. Penrhos, approximately 2 miles west of Caerphilly - Barry Railway junction and RR exchange sidings.
24. Merthyr Express 27/06/1914 – Bedwellty UDC granted license for Rhymney – Caerphilly bus services.
25. The Railway Gazette – Special War Transportation Number, 2nd Edition 2013 (first published 1920), Stockport. 46 were not initially taken over - some were taken over later according to strategic needs.
26. In 1911 France sent troops to Morocco. In response the German Government sent a warship to the port of Agadir to show the French they would have the Germans to reckon with if they occupied. The British Government's response, expressed through the First Lord of the Admiralty, Winston Churchill, was to reinforce the determination to retain a 'healthy naval superiority over Germany'. Sharma, S. 'A History of Britain – The Fate of Empire 1776-2000,' London, 2002.
27. The Railway Gazette op. cit.
28. Clapper, C.F. 'Sir Herbert Walker's Southern Railway,' London, 1973.
29. Clapper, op. cit.
30. The personnel and number of managers on the committee varied through the war.
31. Bell, R. 'History of the British Railways During the War 1939-45,' London, 1948.
32. Merthyr Express 24/02/1917.
33. Caerphilly Journal 15/03/1917.
34. The National Archive ZLIB 10/8 GWR War Reports of the General Manager to the Board of Directors 1914-19. – 09/10/1914.
35. Merthyr Express 08/08/1914.
36. Caerphilly Journal 10/09/1914.
37. Edwards, E.E. 'Echoes of Rhymney,' Newport, 1974.
38. TNA ZLIB 10/8 op. cit. and Merthyr Express 08/08/1914.
39. Turton, K. 'Admiralty Coal Traffic During the First World War: The Jellicoe Trains Part 1,' Railway Archive No. 19, June 2008, Witney, Oxon.
40. Merthyr Express 08/08/1914.
41. Merthyr Express 27/03/1915.
42. Merthyr Express 08/08/1914.
43. TNA ZLIB 10/8 op. cit.
44. Mostly derived from TNA RAIL 583/10 and RAIL 583/11.
45. Merthyr Express 28/09/1918.
46. Merthyr Express 28/09/1918.
47. GWR Magazine January 1917.
48. Merthyr Express 23/03/1918.
49. The Railway Gazette op. cit.
50. Merthyr Express 08/04/1916.
51. Caerphilly Journal 08/04/1915.
52. Caerphilly Journal 13/05/1916.
53. Merthyr Express 17/11/1917.
54. GWR Magazine 1916, p201.
55. Merthyr Express 11/08/1917.
56. Caerphilly Journal 11/03/1915.
57. Caerphilly Journal 13/01/1916.
58. REC Control continued until August 1921.
59. Merthyr Express 12/04/1919.

60 Merthyr Express 12/02/1916.

61 Caerphilly Journal 05/07/1917.

62 Clements, J. 'William Dean – the greatest of them all'. Southampton, 2012.

63 Allcock, N.J. et al. 'The Locomotives of the Great Western Railway, Part 9 standard Two-cylinder classes,' Solihull, 1962.

64 Merthyr Express 09/06/1917.

65 TNA RAIL 583/11.

66 Allcock, N.J. et al. Op. cit. and TNA ZLIB 10/8.

67 Merthyr Express 26/02/1916.

68 Merthyr Express 05/02/1916.

69 Turton, K. op. cit. quoting South Wales Coal Annual, 1914.

70 Turton, K. op. cit.

71 Use of rail links with the ports was eschewed, the Scottish railways serving them, being mainly single track, lacked the capacity for such traffic, in addition to other wartime special traffic carried.

72 TNA RAIL 583/64 – RR Register of Reports of Accidents to Board of Trade, no.2.

73 Named after Admiral of the Fleet Sir John Jellicoe.

74 TNA RAIL 925/121 – GWR Service Timetables No. 10 April 1918.

75 Turton, K. op. cit.

76 Merthyr Express 24/11/1917.

77 TNA ZLIB 10/8 op. cit.

78 Merthyr Express 13/04/1918.

79 Merthyr Express 01/06/1918.

80 Merthyr Express 22/06/1918.

81 Merthyr Express 21/09/1918.

82 Cooke, R.A. 'Track Layout Diagrams of the GWR & BR(WR), Section 47B Vale of Neath, Part 2'. Harwell, Oxon 1981.

83 Jones, D.W.T. 'Talyllyn to Merthyr – A Railway of Life,' Merthyr Tydfil, 2012.

84 Turton, K. op. cit.

85 TNA ZLIB 10/10 Pratt, E.A. 'War Record of the GWR', London, 1921.

86 Turton, K. op. cit.

87 Turton, K. op. cit.

88 Coal carrying ships – not miners!

89 Merthyr Express 10/06/1916.

90 Merthyr Express 05/08/1916.

91 Merthyr Express 12/08/1916.

92 Caerphilly Journal 10/08/1916.

93 Merthyr Express 02/12/1916.

94 Appointed after the BoT took control of all UK coal mines in February 1917.

95 TNA ZLIB 10/8 op. cit. 11/01/1918.

96 Clapper, op. cit.

97 The Railway Gazette op. cit.

98 Merthyr Express 07/07/1917. Tends to contradict other sources claiming Cyfarthfa re-opened in 1915.

99 TNA ZLIB 10/8 op. cit. 05/07/1918.

100 TNA ZLIB 10/8 op. cit. 10/03/1916. L&Y and NER – Lancashire & Yorkshire and North Eastern Railways respectively.

101 Orders in Council - issued "by and with the advice of His/Her Majesty's Privy Council" … to transfer powers from Ministers of the UK government to … 'other government bodies.' www.parliament.uk .

102 TNA ZLIB 10/8 op. cit. 20/04/1917.

103 Merthyr Express 06/10/1917, 13/10/1917, 22/12/1917, 12/01/1918, 26/01/1918.

104 Merthyr Express 12/06/1915.

105 Shore, L. 'Peerless Powell Duffryn,' Lydney, 2012. Proportion of Rhymney Valley miners unknown.

106 Merthyr Express 07/09/1918.

107 TNA ZLIB 10/8 – 19/03/1915.

108 TNA RAIL 583/11 – 06/12/1918.

109 Merthyr Express 26/02/1916.

110 Merthyr Express 05/02/1916.

111 TNA RAIL 583/10, 01/01/1915 & 03/12/1915 respectively.

112 Merthyr Express 14/12/1918.

113 McCarthy, T. 'David Bowen B. & M.R. Driver – His Log Summer 1916,' WRRC Archive, 2014?

114 Merthyr Express 27/03/1915.

115 TNA RAIL 583/11 – 03/05/1918. Patent fuel – combination of coal dust and tar to form a 'brick' of coal.

116 TNA RAIL 583/10 and RAIL 583/11.

117 Bryan, T. 'The Great Western Railway – A Celebration,' Hersham, Surrey, 2010.

118 Merthyr Express 30/12/1916.

119 Merthyr Express 10/06/1916.

120 Merthyr Express 01/04/1916.

121 TNA RAIL/10 – 07/04/1916.

122 Merthyr Express 19/01/1918.

123 Merthyr Express 01/09/1918.

124 Merthyr Express 15/09/1918.

125 Merthyr Express 26/02/1916.

126 Merthyr Express 27/10/1917 & 12/10/1918.

127 TNA RAIL 65/10 Director's Minute Book, 1912-22.

128 Merthyr Express 13/05/1916.

129 Merthyr Express 19/08/1916.

130 Merthyr Express 12/02/1916.

131 Merthyr Express 12/10/1918.

132 Merthyr Express 10/02/1917.

133 TNA RAIL 583/64 – 10/08/1915.

134 TNA RAIL 583/64 – 28/10/1916.

135 TNA RAIL 583/64 – 20/01/1917- 'motor train' - carriage incorporating a small steam operated power unit.

136 Bryan, T. Op. cit.

137 TNA ZLIB 10/10 Op. cit.

138 The Railway Gazette Op. cit.

139 Shore,L.. Op. cit.

140 Mitchell, V. & Smith, K, 'Pontypool to Mountain Ash', Midhurst, Sussex, 2005.

141 Merthyr Express & Caerphilly Journal, 24/05/1917.

142 Caerphilly Journal 05/07/1917, Merthyr Express 15/05/1920

143 Caerphilly Journal 27/05/1915.

144 Merthyr Express 05/06/1920.